IELTS Speaking Mastercl

Proven Strategies for an 8+ Band Score

by Charles Hooton

For Hitesh

TABLE OF CONTENTS

Preface..1

Introduction...3

The speaking test format..5

Scoring and the band descriptors...6

Fluency and coherence...7

Lexical resource...24

Grammatical range and accuracy...32

Pronunciation..44

Part One...53

Part Two and the **Narrative+Six system**...74

    People...85

    Places...108

    Things...133

    Experiences and Events...165

Part three...187

Appendix One - Fifty useful phrasal verbs..201

Appendix Two - Fifty useful idioms..217

And Finally...241

PREFACE

One of my earliest IELTS students was a young man called Arun from India. During our first Skype meeting, he explained that he had a first-class bachelor's degree in computer science and now wanted to study for a master's in Britain. His dream was to secure a place at Oxford University.

It was obvious that he has a brilliant mind and would have had no problem getting accepted had it not been for one big problem. Oxford required him to have an overall score of 7.5 in the IELTS examination with a minimum of 7.0 in each of the four components. Arun told me that he had already taken the test twice and achieved the required overall grade of 7.5 on both occasions. The obstacle, however, was his speaking score. He couldn't get above a 6.0.

Arun was understandably frustrated and was on the verge of giving up on his big dream. His spoken English was good, certainly better than a 6.0 I thought, and so we spent time trying to analyse what the problem was. The total unpredictability of part two of the speaking test unnerved him, but what he disliked the most was the fact that he didn't know precisely what the examiners wanted. The published band descriptors were, for him, too vague. To get a top grade for grammatical range and accuracy you are told to *'use a full range of structures naturally and appropriately.'*

What Arun wanted to know was exactly what structures he needed to use. There is, however, no simple answer to this question. The band descriptors are vague for a reason. The examiners don't want to provide a list of grammatical structures for you to learn and repeat mechanically because they prefer, instead, to hear which ones you use naturally in your ordinary conversation. Ultimately, IELTS is not a test of your grammar but you need to have excellent grammar to do well in it.

We do, however, know what types of structures proficient speakers of English use in conversation and we also know which ones you are expected to be familiar with at the CEFR levels of B1, B2, & C1 etc.

What Arun wanted was a strategy to incorporate these structures into his conversation naturally. He has a very logical and analytical mind, and he wanted a step-by-step method. And so I set out to develop one for him.

The result was what we called the *Narrative+Six* system and it's a methodical approach to the IELTS speaking test, especially the challenging part two. It worked for Arun and I had the pleasure of meeting him personally in Oxford a couple of years after our first Skype call. Since then it has been used by many other students most of whom have succeeded in raising their speaking score by one point or more.

In this book, I will share the system with you and I sincerely hope that you will achieve similar success. People only take the IELTS exam because they are pursuing a dream and I wish you all the very best in yours.

INTRODUCTION

The IELTS examination has become the world's most important English language exam. Three million tests are taken every year in 140 countries and the numbers are increasing. However, IELTS differs from many other popular English language exams in two significant ways. First, candidates usually sit the exam only if they have a specific reason for doing so. It is therefore unlike the highly popular Cambridge exams such as KET, PET, and CPE which are often taken as a matter of routine by students at schools or in higher education.

Second, unlike many exams, IELTS is impossible to fail. You will receive a band score from 1.0 to 9.0 with the former equating to a *non-user* of English and the latter meaning that you are *an expert user*. Scores are given as whole numbers or in 0.5 increments. In addition to an overall band score, you will be awarded a further score, again as whole numbers or 0.5 increments, for each of the four elements: writing, listening, reading, and speaking. The overall band score is the average for these four parts.

The reasons why people take the IELTS exam vary enormously but they usually fall into one of three categories: immigration, study, and work. The scores required also vary greatly but I have noticed over the years that they have been rising, and examples of employers and institutions lowering their requirements have been remarkably few.

Another difference I have noted in recent years is that minimum band scores are invariably required in each of the four papers. Once upon a time, some institutions were content to see merely an overall band score of, let's say 7.0, and were not too concerned if you achieved this by performing well in the reading or listening elements and effectively subsidising a poor speaking result. Rarely is this now possible.

Essentially, there is little value nowadays in achieving an overall score of less than 7.0 and also not falling below that figure in any of the four papers. This is what many UK universities require for postgraduate study. The General Medical Council in the UK is a little more strict and asks for an overall 7.5 with no paper below 7.0. To get maximum points for English language ability in your application for Australian citizenship you need to achieve at least 8.0 in each paper.

And here is the biggest problem for the IELTS student. In my experience, many good candidates tend to score well in the listening and reading papers but underperform in the writing and speaking parts. I have lost count of the number of students who have come to me having already taken the exam and have achieved 8.5 for listening but only 6.5 for speaking. They have come to me because they need at least 7.0 in each paper.

We will leave the discussion of the writing paper for another book but there are, I believe, three clear reasons why many students underperform in the speaking exam.

The first, and perhaps the most obvious is that this is the only part of the exam where you are faced with an examiner. Most of us would much prefer to take a multiple-choice paper-based exam than have to speak to a person in authority we have never met before. Inevitably we become nervous and, in extreme cases, this may turn into a crippling tongue-tied anxiety.

The second reason for underperformance is the lack of time. In the reading paper, you have an hour and you have some choice on how to use that time. You can spend more time on a part you find more difficult and you have the opportunity to reflect, revise and change your mind. This is simply not possible in the 11-14 minutes of the speaking test. You can't sit and think for five minutes before answering a question, and there is no going back. You have to get it right the first time.

So many of my students have told me how quickly the speaking test seemed to flash by. In one sense this is a good thing, your agony is not prolonged. However, it does mean that every second counts. Every word and every sentence must be productive and geared towards your aim of impressing the examiner with your fluency, your extensive vocabulary, and your knowledge of grammatical structures. For every student who expressed surprise about the speed of the test at least one other has said something along the lines of, *I wish I had said* ....

And finally, the band descriptors document is somewhat vague. It does not, for example, tell you precisely what type of grammatical structures and pronunciation features you should be using.

However, with the right preparation, you won't be one of those underperforming students. Being familiar with the format of the test, knowing what the examiner is looking for, rehearsing sample answers to frequently asked questions, and using my *Narrative+Six* system could mean achieving a half or full-point increase in your speaking band score. That, for many students, could secure a university place, an offer of work, or be accepted for immigration.

THE SPEAKING TEST FORMAT

I assume that if you are at the stage of reading this book then you are aware of the format of the IELTS speaking test. You may also have studied the official IELTS website - ielts.org - where you will find a description of the speaking test and the other three modules of the exam. If you haven't already done so I would thoroughly recommend looking at this invaluable site.

If you are at a very early stage of preparation for the exam, however, here is a brief overview of the speaking test.

It will last for approximately 11 to 14 minutes and will be recorded. There are three distinct parts as follows:

Part one:

This will last for four to five minutes and the examiner will ask a number of general questions about your family, daily life, and whether you work or study.

Part two:

The examiner will give you a card which gives details of a particular topic you must talk about. You will be given a minute to prepare for this and you may make notes if you wish. You should then speak for up to two minutes after which the examiner may ask a couple of questions based on what you have said.

Part three:

For the final four to five minutes the examiner will ask further questions related to the topic in part two. It is an opportunity for you to show that you are able to discuss more abstract issues and express opinions in a speculative way.

(Please note that the speaking test is the same for both versions of the IELTS exam, Academic and General Training.)

SCORING AND THE BAND DESCRIPTORS

The IELTS speaking exam is marked according to four band descriptors.

Fluency and coherence	How fluently you speak and how well your opinions and arguments are connected.
Lexical resource	How varied, precise, and error-free your vocabulary is.
Grammatical range and accuracy	How varied and error-free your grammar is.
Pronunciation	How clear and comprehensible your pronunciation is.

For each of the four, you will be given a mark ranging from 1 to 9 (there are no 0.5 increments, only whole numbers.) The four are then averaged to obtain your final speaking score.

It is possible that the four marks when averaged will result in a fraction. For example, 7 8 6 6 will give an average of 6.75. This will be rounded up, so you would be given 7.0 overall.

8 7 6 4 gives an average of 6.25 which will be rounded up to give you a final overall speaking score of 6.5.

It is crucial that you don't neglect any one of the four components during your preparation and the test itself. You might speak with superb pronunciation and use a fairly wide range of vocabulary and grammatical structures scoring you an 8.0 and two 7.0s. However your arguments are insufficiently coherent, and the examiner gives only a 5.0 for this descriptor. Your overall score will, therefore, be 6.5.

The purpose of this book is to give you the tools you will need to score at least 7.0 in the speaking test. For many candidates, any score lower than this won't be sufficient for their purposes. Therefore, in the following chapters, we will look only at the band descriptors at 7.0 and above.

FLUENCY AND COHERENCE

To achieve high marks for fluency and coherence you will need, according to the band descriptors, to do the following.

Band 7

- *speak at length without noticeable effort or loss of coherence*

- *may demonstrate language-related hesitation at times, or some repetition and/or self-correction*

- *use a range of connectives and discourse markers with some flexibility*

Band 8

- *speak fluently with only occasional repetition or self-correction; hesitation is usually content-related and only rarely to search for language*

- *develop topics coherently and appropriately*

Band 9

- *speak fluently with only rare repetition or self-correction;*

- *any hesitation is content-related rather than to find words or grammar*

- *speak coherently with fully appropriate cohesive features*

- *develop topics fully and appropriately*

(The speaking descriptors for all bands are available on the official ielts.org website.)

Fluency

Fluency, for the purposes of IELTS, is the ability to speak naturally and accurately. It doesn't necessarily mean that you have to be perfect, but you should have a sufficiently good command of English so that you don't interrupt your speaking with long pauses or awkward gaps. A fluent speaker also rarely self-corrects. This means that you shouldn't be making mistakes, then realising that you have made an error and having a second attempt at getting it right.

Fluency is something that comes naturally with practice so ideally, you should try to engage in conversation as often as possible. However, there are a few tips and techniques that should help your patterns of speech sound more like those of a native speaker.

Thinking in English

As you go about your normal day try to take as many opportunities as possible to think about what you are seeing and observing but in English. Look at people on the bus or train and describe them as fully as you can as if you are speaking to another person. Do the same with buildings, trees, flowers, and, in fact, anything that you encounter in your daily routine. Don't forget the intangible things. Tell your invisible friend how you are feeling and what mood you are in.

You will find this a little strange at first and also quite difficult, but persistence will yield enormous benefits. It is only when you start thinking in a second language that you are well on your way to fluency.

Slowing down

It is a common misconception that fluent speakers of a language speak quickly. It might sound as though they are when you are trying to learn their language and trying to understand them, but in reality, most native English speakers don't speak particularly rapidly. Try to watch news programmes in English and pay special attention to the speed at which the presenters speak. Record a short section of a few minutes in length and practice repeating it at the same pace.

Don't worry about mistakes

Some candidates have the opposite problem of speaking too quickly. Because they are so concerned about making mistakes, they try to think of exactly the right grammatical construction and, as a result, they speak far too slowly. You will, unfortunately, be penalised and lose marks for this. It is highly likely that you will lose more marks than had you maintained a normal speaking speed and made the occasional mistake. Your mistakes in the IELTS written exam will be noticed and your grades will be adjusted accordingly. This won't always happen in the spoken test.

Choose a filler word

If you do find yourself hesitating because you are desperately thinking about what to say next, then don't be afraid to use the occasional filler word such as *umm* and *ahh*.

If anything this will make you sound more fluent than less because native speakers use these fillers all the time.

Don't become anxious about content

I know that many students become very anxious about the questions they are likely to be asked, especially in part two of the IELTS test. This anxiety, combined with a type of part two question they are totally unprepared for, leads to the student speaking far too slowly and losing fluency as they desperately think of something to say. Remember that IELTS is a test of English. It is not a general knowledge test nor is it an intelligence test. Therefore evading the topic on the part two cue card and talking about something else is a better tactic than speaking incredibly slowly because you are desperately trying to think of something to say.

Practice

Nothing is better for helping you get a really good band score for fluency than practice and lots of it. I appreciate, however, that for some students finding speaking partners is not easy. However, don't make the mistake of thinking that a speaking partner has to have a similar or better level of English than you. Nor do they have to be experts in IELTS and be able to correct your errors. Anybody who has a basic knowledge of English and is prepared to sit and listen to you is better than nobody at all. It genuinely will make a huge difference to your fluency if you are able to devote time to answering part two sample cue cards even if the person you are speaking to is unable to detect your mistakes.

If there genuinely isn't anybody in your town who is able to help, then try looking online. There are a number of websites that offer language exchange and it should be possible to arrange to chat by Skype. There are also Facebook pages that connect students wanting IELTS speaking partners.

Coherence

Coherence is, at its simplest, the ability to make sense. You need to express your ideas in a logical way so that the examiner has absolutely no doubt that you have understood the question. You stay on topic and are able to connect your sentences in such a way that the listener can easily follow and comprehend your argument or opinion. The key to this is the correct use of discourse markers and linking devices. Some resources treat these two as the same thing but there are minor differences, so I will look at them separately.

Discourse markers

Discourse markers and filler words share similarities. Neither adds much in the way of meaning to what you are saying, and filler words add virtually nothing. If I were to ask you to talk about your favourite type of tree and you began with a long *ummm* noise, I would assume that you were thinking about what to say. If the *ummm* was very long I could safely assume that you knew very little about any type of tree. The *ummm* is a filler and is there just to avoid silence.

Discourse markers, on the other hand, are slightly different in that they do more than fill gaps. They have the function of helping to manage the flow and structure of speech. If again I were to ask you to speak about your favourite type of tree but this time you started your answer with *well*, then I would assume that you had thought about my question and were prepared with an answer.

The following discourse makers are the most common in spoken English:

well	*okay*	*right*	*so*	*like*
actually	*I mean*	*you know*	*mind you*	*anyway*

Well, okay, right & so

As we have seen, *well* can be a way to start an answer to a question. But, in addition, *okay*, *right* and *so* have much the same function and all four are commonly used by native speakers. Essentially, they signal to the listener that you have considered the question and are prepared with an answer. All four are perfectly acceptable and appropriate to use in the IELTS spoken test; just be careful not to use the same one for every question.

Examiner:
What is your favourite season of the year?

Candidate:
Okay, it's definitely summer because ...
Well, it's definitely summer because ...
Right, it's definitely summer because ...
So, it's definitely summer because ...

Like

Although there is evidence of the word *like* being used as a discourse marker since the nineteenth century, it is only relatively recently that its use has massively increased.

This phenomenon, and its rapid spread across the English-speaking world, has been the subject of academic interest and scholarly articles.

Some have attributed its success to the popular American situation comedy *Friends* whose six principal characters added *like* to most of their conversations. In the last couple of decades, its use has spread from the young to people of all age groups and all social groups.

Though some academics have dismissed the overuse of *like* as a characteristic of careless speech, its occasional appearance in your IELTS spoken test is acceptable. It will certainly show that you are familiar with how native speakers use the language.

But, as with all discourse markers, don't overdo it, particularly this one.

The first thing to note with *like* as a discourse marker is that it has nothing to do with the verb *like*. Nor does it have any connection to *like* as a noun - as in a Facebook *like*. It has no meaning but, as with all discourse markers, merely sends a signal to your listener.

Consider the following question and answer to an IELTS part one question:

Examiner:
What is the most important birthday in your country?

Candidate:
When my grandparents were young, I'm fairly sure it was the twenty-first, but now it's definitely the eighteenth birthday. It's like such a big thing to have a huge celebration with all your family and friends when you get to that age.

Here *like* is signalling that the speaker is going to elaborate on his or her point and clarify the first statement.

And here it is again performing the same function in another IELTS part one answer.

Examiner:
What benefits can people get from sunshine?

Candidate:
I understand that exposure to the sun, as long as you take precautions, can have some health benefits, in particular, helping your body to produce vitamin D. But for me, it's like so important for helping enhance your mood. Everyone seems happier on a sunny day.

Another use of *like* is to signal exaggeration, as in the following:

Examiner:
Tell me about a place near water that you enjoy visiting.

Candidate:
There's a hidden lake in the middle of an area of dense woodland quite near to where my grandparents live. It's quite high up amongst the hills and it's like the most beautiful place you've ever seen.

Actually

Actually, as a discourse marker, has a couple of uses. Its first signals to the listener that the speaker is about to convey surprising or unexpected information.

Examiner:
What is your favourite season of the year?

Candidate:
Actually, it's winter because ...

Summer and spring are usually considered the most popular seasons so winter, certainly in the mind of this candidate, is an unexpected answer.

It may also be used to signal a correction of information, as in the following:

Examiner:
Did you learn to play a musical instrument at school?

Candidate:
No, unfortunately, I didn't, and I definitely regret that now. Actually, we did use to bang drums and cymbals in my elementary school but that doesn't really count I suppose.

Mind you

Mind you also performs the function of signalling the fact that you have had an afterthought that contrasts with what you have just said.

Examiner:
Do you enjoy birthdays?

Candidate:
Absolutely, my parents always liked to have big birthday parties for me and also my two siblings when we were growing up and they were great fun. All of us have continued that

tradition. Mind you, we might stop when we get older. I think lavish parties might look a bit silly when you are in your forties.

I mean

I mean signals to the listener that you are about to clarify or add further explanation to a statement, as in the following IELTS part one exchange:

Examiner:
Do you think your neighbourhood is a good place for children?

Candidate:
It's an absolutely wonderful place for kids to grow up, I mean there's hardly any traffic and so very little pollution and there are some beautiful parks in the vicinity.

You know

You know indicates that you are about to, or have just, said something that your listener will already be aware of. You are more likely to use it with people that you know well because you can more easily assume shared knowledge, but it can still be appropriate with people you know less well as in the following answer:

Examiner:
Do you think children should be allowed to watch a lot of television?

Candidate:
Well, there are two sides to this because on the one hand television can be very educational. But, you know, the programmes can often be really low quality and offer nothing more than mindless entertainment.

Anyway

Anyway as a discourse marker may be used to signal the end of a conversation with somebody - *anyway, I must be going because I've got a meeting at three* - but in the context of the IELTS exam, it will most likely be used to signal a change of direction in the topic, particularly in part two. Consider the following cue card and in particular the transition from the *why* to the *what*.

Describe a situation or time when you were late.
You should say:
what you were late for
why you were late
what you did about being late
and explain how you felt about being late

You could do it as in this excerpt from a sample response:

... and it eventually dawned on me that my alarm clock hadn't gone off. It was the first time ever that it hadn't worked properly, and it would have to be on the day of my job interview. Anyway, the first thing I did was to phone my local taxi company ....

Linking Devices

In addition to discourse markers, the appropriate use of linking devices will help you to achieve a high band score in the fluency and coherence category. These devices, quite simply, are words or phrases which show the relationships between the ideas, information, and opinions that you will express in your answers.

We can group the most useful linking devices into the following eight categories:

Indicating contrast

The most commonly used word to indicate contrast is *but* as in this exchange from part one:

Examiner:
What do you think of fast food?

Candidate:
Fast food is certainly very convenient, and it can also be quite cheap which may a big consideration for some people. I personally do enjoy eating the occasional burger and I can't resist French fries but I know they are not exactly healthy and so I don't go to fast food restaurants too often.

Here we start by giving the advantages of fast food and then changing direction to offer a major disadvantage. The word *but* does the job of signalling the contrast. It is, however, an extremely common word and there are these alternatives that perform much the same function:

| in contrast | on the other hand | conversely |

Here are examples of them being used in part one answers:

Examiner:
How do you usually get your news?

Candidate:
These days it is invariably online. When I have a few spare moments during the day I quickly glance at news apps on my smartphone. Sometimes I watch the late evening news when I'm at home in the evening. This is in contrast to only a few years ago when I used to buy a newspaper every day. It's been ages since I last did that.

Examiner:
Do you like your neighbours?

Candidate:
I do like my neighbours. We always make a little small talk if we share the lift. We have also exchanged sets of keys with each other. I trust them enough to do that and it could be useful if I accidentally lock myself out. On the other hand, we do maintain our privacy and it is not as though we are having drinks with them each evening.

Examiner:
Do you like shopping?

Candidate:
It very much depends. I have always very much disliked shopping for clothes. I just find it a tedious chore and I would rather order clothes online. I suppose it's because I don't find clothes particularly interesting. Conversely, I absolutely adore shopping for electronic goods and gadgets like laptops and mobile phones. I often browse in the Apple store in my city even though I can't really afford or need anything new right now.

Indicating concession

There is a difference between indicating a contrast as in the examples above and indicating a concession. With contrast, we are usually comparing a similar aspect of two different people, things, or situations. With concession, we are often contrasting two different aspects of the same person, thing, or situation. Consider the following statement:

Robert loves playing football. David, on the other hand, prefers tennis.

Here we have a simple contrast indicated by the linking device *on the other hand*.

Now look at this statement:

Although David usually prefers to play tennis, today he's playing football with Robert.

This sentence is an example of concession, when something surprising happens - David is playing football today - even though we have conceded something else - that he prefers to play tennis.

The most common concession linking devices are:

however	nevertheless	although	despite	even though

Examiner:
Do you have a hobby?

Candidate:
I absolutely love to play the piano. I started to learn a couple of years ago because I inherited an instrument from my grandmother. However, my big problem is finding the opportunity to practice. Work takes up a huge amount of my time. That's why I wished I had started as a child.

Examiner:
Do you ever ride a bicycle?

Candidate:
I've had a bicycle for many years but the big problem in my city is that many of the roads are really not suitable for bikes. Riding a bike in the rush hour can, therefore, be an alarming and dangerous experience. Nevertheless, I do cycle to and from work every day. It's good exercise and considerably cheaper than using my car.

Examiner:

Do you think the clothes a person wears are important?

Candidate:

No, I don't, and I believe you should be judged not on what you choose to wear but on how you act and what you say. I dislike dressing up in what other people think are smart clothes for special occasions such as job interviews, although the last time I went to an interview I did put on a suit and tie. Sometimes we have to wear what other people expect irrespective of our own personal views.

Examiner:

Which city has been your favourite holiday destination?

Candidate:

Last year my wife and I went to Lisbon for the first time. We were only there for three days and it rained pretty much all the time. Despite the weather we still loved it. We didn't do as much walking as we had planned but there are historic trams running through the most picturesque parts of the city and so we still got to see a lot. And, of course, the rain didn't spoil our enjoyment of the traditional Portuguese restaurants.

Examiner:

Do you like the same fruits and vegetables today as you did when you were a child?

Candidate:

I do like the same fruits that I ate when I was young. My grandfather grew lots of fruit, particularly strawberries and blackberries and he also had apple and pear trees. He lived only a few doors away and so we had a constant supply of really fresh and delicious fruit. Vegetables were a different matter. Even though he grew these too, I hated them. I really struggled with things like cabbage and broccoli. It's strange how your tastes change when you are older. I enjoy vegetables now.

Giving examples

In all three parts of the exam, you will need to expand on your answers by providing examples and giving evidence to back up your statements. This is certainly true of part one where it is easy, because of the nature of the questions, to give far too short a response. If you remember always to give examples, then it is likely that the length will be correct.

The most common and useful linking devices for this purpose are:

| for instance | for example | such as | in particular | namely |

Examiner:
What is there for a tourist to see in your hometown?

Candidate:
We don't get a lot of tourists and I think that's mainly because we are too far away from the capital. And I think that's a pity because there are a lot of very interesting things to see. For instance, the castle dates back to the tenth century and is remarkably well preserved considering its turbulent history. The cathedral too is a very ancient structure and is considered one of the most beautiful churches in the country.

Examiner:
What would you change about your home if you could?

Candidate:
There are a few things that I would quite like to change over the next couple of years if I can afford it. One is merely cosmetic, I would love a new kitchen. There's nothing actually wrong with the one we have but it's looking a little old-fashioned. The other changes would be a better use of our money because they would be a long-term investment, for example installing a more efficient central heating system and also replacing the windows with double-glazed units.

Examiner:
What jobs do people do in your hometown?

Candidate:
Originally the town was the centre of the region's coal mining industry and there were a number of mines that employed many workers. That's all changed because most of these places have closed. Nowadays the biggest employers are contact centres and huge depots for online retailers. Young people who don't have the opportunity to go to university now do low-skilled jobs such as dealing with customer queries or dispatching orders.

Examiner:

What kind of art do you like?

Candidate:

If we are talking about paintings, then I'm a bit of a traditionalist. In particular, I much prefer the works of the old masters of Renaissance Italy to the abstract works of the twentieth century. I would much prefer to look at a beautiful landscape or portraits of people than a lot of the abstract works I've seen in museums which just seem to consist of splashes of colour.

Examiner:

What kind of clothes do you prefer to wear?

Candidate:

Unfortunately, I have to dress quite smartly for work which means a suit and a tie and that's certainly not what I would choose to wear. Ideally, I like to dress for comfort rather than style or fashion. So that means what I think is referred to as leisure wear, namely tracksuits and trainers and anything that is loose-fitting and comfortable.

Showing similarity

Another way to expand your responses in all parts of the speaking test is to show similarity and you can do this by using the following transitions and conjunctions:

likewise	similarly	in the same way

Examiner:

Do you think children can benefit from going to art galleries?

Candidate:

When I was young my parents made a point of taking me to galleries and museums. I must admit that sometimes I was bored and would have preferred to have gone to the beach or an amusement park. However, I'm very glad that they did because I think it was the foundation for the interest in art that I now have. Looking at art makes me think and reflect and I think it boosts my creativity. Likewise, I'm sure it has similar effects on the young.

Examiner:

When do you usually get up in the morning?

Candidate:

During the week I invariably have to be in college by nine and because I need to shower, have breakfast, make my sandwiches for lunch, and then catch a bus, it means that I really need to be out of bed by seven at the latest. Similarly at the weekend; I don't actually need to get up that early but I have found that I am much more productive in the mornings and so I still get out of bed at seven. I don't need to set an alarm because my body clock is so used to my morning routine.

Examiner:

Do you think there should be restrictions on the use of the internet by children?

Candidate:

Oh absolutely. The internet can be hugely beneficial, but it can also be quite dangerous. You can't be absolutely sure about the identity of people when online and children don't have the experience to understand that some might be intent on doing them harm. So I think that parents do need to monitor carefully what their children are looking at online in the same way that they should know what people they talk to and mix with when they are not at home.

Showing result

It is in part three of the test that you are most likely to use the result linking devices. Here you will be required to expand on your arguments and discuss more abstract issues. The conclusion of your argument will benefit from the use of one of the following devices:

therefore	as a result	thus	consequently	as a consequence

The examples are all from part three of the test.

Examiner:

Should co-workers also spend their leisure time together?

Candidate:

It is inevitable that co-workers will spend some time together after work. When I was an intern in a large company, members of my team often used to go to a bar or cafe at the end of the day and almost always after work on a Friday. In some respects, it was good for morale and had a positive effect on teamwork when we were back in the office. There is a potential problem though, and this is something that I definitely experienced, and it's the difficulty of maintaining a hierarchical structure in a social setting. When you are all out drinking in the evening, and particularly if the boss is with you, there is a tendency for respect and deference to break down. Therefore you may have problems re-establishing them when you are back in the office on Monday morning.

Examiner:

How are the eating habits now in your country different from eating habits in the past?

Candidate:

A couple of generations ago it was common for all members of a family to eat together at set times. In particular, the evening meal was the focal point of the day. Everyone would sit at the dining table and discuss what they had been doing that day and nobody would leave until everyone had finished. And then the children would do the washing up. Nowadays most women work and don't have time to prepare a big meal and members of families often have different timetables. They don't all come home at the same time. As a result, what happens now is that people help themselves to whatever is in the fridge or put something in the microwave. They don't have the opportunity to sit and eat together.

Examiner:

What is your opinion of the way languages are taught in schools?

Candidate:

I'm afraid that I don't have a particularly high opinion of language teaching in schools in my country, although I can only really speak from personal experience. The biggest problem is that the foreign language, in my case English, was taught in much the same way as history or geography. We were given lots of facts that we were meant to remember. We sat and wrote out grammatical rules which we had to memorise and then in exams we had to write essays to show that we knew how to use them. Very rarely did we actually practice speaking the language and thus the first time I visited an English-speaking country I was inadequately prepared. I had no problem reading the newspapers but had major difficulties holding a conversation.

Examiner:
How do most people travel long distances in your country?

Candidate:
In the fairly recent past, most people travelled long distances by train. My grandparents did have a car but for holidays they invariably took the long-distance trains because they were frequent, reliable, and, most important, comparatively cheap. It was a lot less expensive and less troublesome than driving to a distant place. Nobody ever flew anywhere because air travel was only for the very rich. But in the last couple of decades, low-cost airlines have started to operate from many of the smaller regional airports and it's now cheaper to fly from one part of the country to another than it is to go by rail. Consequently not only do people use planes more than trains but they also travel a lot more than they did in the past.

Examiner:
How are education priorities today different from those in the past?

Candidate:
I think that in my parents' day, the chief object of school was seen as providing students with a solid all-round education that would prepare them for life in the outside world. To a certain extent that is still true but increasingly the focus has become the passing of exams and in particular an obsession with grades. Everybody assumes that you won't get a decent job unless you go to one of the best universities and to do that you need to get high grades in particular exams. As a consequence, I feel that some of our schools are more like exam factories and they are obsessed with targets and benchmarks instead of providing a good general level of education.

Indicating sequence

And finally, there will be occasions, particularly in part three of the test, when it is appropriate to indicate a sequence of events or ideas. There are a large number of expressions that you can use to indicate sequence, but the following are perhaps the most useful:

first or *firstly*	*second* or *secondly*	*next* or *then*	*finally* or *lastly*

Examiner:

Why is it important to protect the natural environment?

Candidate:

First I think it is important for our general well-being. Lots of people, like me, work in quite stressful jobs in busy and often polluted cities and it's important to have the opportunity at weekends and holidays to go into the countryside and relax in a beautiful environment. Second, scientists constantly tell us how important biodiversity is and that a healthy natural environment is vitally important for all ecosystems. And finally, I think we owe it to future generations to protect the environment. We are merely its custodians and we have a duty to pass it on to our children for them to appreciate and benefit from.

LEXICAL RESOURCE

Lexical resource refers to your ability to use a wide range of vocabulary accurately and appropriately.

Let's start by looking at the descriptors for bands 7, 8, & 9 to establish precisely what the examiner will be listening for.

Band 7

- *uses vocabulary resource flexibly to discuss a variety of topics*

- *uses some less common and idiomatic vocabulary and shows some awareness of style and collocation, with some inappropriate choices*

- *uses paraphrase effectively*

Band 8

- *uses a wide vocabulary resource readily and flexibly to convey precise meaning*

- *uses less common and idiomatic vocabulary skilfully, with occasional inaccuracies*

- *uses paraphrase effectively as required*

Band 9

- *uses vocabulary with full flexibility and precision in all topics*

- *uses idiomatic language naturally and accurately*

We can see from these descriptors that, for the purposes of IELTS, lexical resource comprises three key areas, vocabulary, idioms, and paraphrasing. In this chapter, we will examine each in detail and look at strategies to improve your scores.

Vocabulary

Nobody knows for sure how many words there are in the English language. New words are being created all the time and many become obsolete. One source, the Global Language Monitor, estimates that there are a little over a million English words. A more useful and interesting statistic is that the average well-educated native English speaker will have a vocabulary of about 20,000 words. However, what is even more interesting is that this average speaker will only use about 1,000 words in ordinary daily conversations. And it is pretty much the same in most languages - we use only a small fraction of the words that we actually know.

It is for this reason that a native speaker won't necessarily perform well in the IELTS speaking test. If the examiner asks him what he likes to do in the evenings, he will possibly respond by saying something along the lines of, '*I like to go to the gym.*'

It's what he would say to a friend or colleague. He would assume that the friend genuinely wanted to know and would respond in a direct and straightforward way.

IELTS examiners, however, are different. They don't really want to know what you like to do in the evenings. All they are interested in is how you will answer the question, what vocabulary and grammar you will use, and whether it is coherent and makes sense. Your primary aim, therefore, is to impress the examiner and you won't do it by using the verb *like*. It's too common and is the type of word used by a band 5 candidate. This brings us to the subject of:

Synonyms

Some students think that learning long lists of synonyms for commonly used words is enough to obtain a good band score, but it is not necessarily a good tactic. If we look at the band descriptors, we can see that at band eight you need to use, *a wide vocabulary resource readily and flexibly to convey precise meaning.*

And this is the problem. Some synonyms are simply inappropriate and may do the very opposite of conveying precise meaning. Let's imagine that the examiner asks you about your favourite restaurant. You want to say that the food is good but realise that this is too common a word and unlikely to impress. You need a synonym and there are many available for the word *good*. How about telling the examiner that the food in your favourite restaurant is *congenial*?

The problem with this synonym is that although it does imply that something is good, we use it in only certain contexts. It's perfectly possible to say that you enjoy this particular restaurant because the staff are *congenial*, and you would be likely to impress the examiner if you did so. The adjective *congenial* is almost always used in connection with people. It means that they are pleasant and agreeable. We don't, however, use it when describing food. It's not appropriate, it sounds strange and the examiner will know that you don't know how to use it correctly.

A far better way to learn new vocabulary instead of memorising lists of synonyms is to see and learn the words in context. By far the best method of doing this is by reading, and this is a step-by-step way of approaching this.

1. Pick an IELTS part two question. There are plenty in chapter seven.

2. Go to the website of a reputable English-language newspaper and search for articles connected with the topic.

3. Underline any new words and write them down in a notebook. Include dictionary meanings and, most importantly, their context. Write the whole sentence from the newspaper so that you can memorise how the new word is used.

4. Regularly review your notes to help you to remember the new vocabulary.

5. If you get the opportunity, try to use these words when speaking and writing.

Connotation

A significant advantage of learning new words from articles rather than from lists of synonyms is that you will use these words with proper connotations. Words have both a literal meaning and a suggestive one and a high-performing IELTS candidate will be aware of the differences.

Words can have one of three connotations - positive, negative, and neutral. An example often given is three adjectives to describe a person who is the opposite of fat.

Negative connotation	Neutral connotation	Positive connotation
skinny	*thin*	*slim*

If you, as an IELTS candidate are asked to describe your closest friend and you say that she is *thin*, the examiner won't be able to infer any further meaning from your statement. If, however, you say that she is *skinny* he will know that you really think that she is too thin. This word has negative connotations. On the other hand, if you say that your friend is *slim* the examiner will know that you think favourably of her body size. *Slim* has very positive connotations, it infers that you think that somebody is thin but in an attractive and favourable way.

Collocations

A further advantage of building your vocabulary from articles is that you will also learn how English words are collocated. Most people in the early stages of studying English are made aware of the fact that native speakers say *strong wind* and *heavy rain*. If you say *heavy wind* it sounds quite strange.

To achieve at least a band 7.0 you are required to show some awareness of collocation but with occasional mistakes. If you want to achieve greater than 7.0 in your speaking, then you must ensure that your collocations are effortless and accurate. One of the most effective ways to build your lists of collocations is by reading articles from newspapers and magazines, but you can also make use of two excellent resources to find specific examples to help you in the IELTS exam.

The first, and best, is the Oxford Collocations Dictionary. This is available as a physical book and there is also an online version which you can subscribe to. As an alternative learn how to make use of ozdic.com. This is a superb free resource that is useful to all students of English at advanced levels, not just those studying for IELTS.

Tips for using a collocation dictionary

1. Choose a topic

The best way to use collocation dictionaries is thematically. Choose a topic that you know regularly crops up in the exam. There are many in the chapters to follow but, for now, we'll look at the subject of holidays which is an IELTS favourite.

After you have typed in the word *holiday* in the search bar you will receive a list of words that collocate with it and these are arranged according to grammatical function, whether they are adjectives, nouns, or verbs etc.

2. Make notes of the collocations you might use

As you prepare for the exam you will become familiar with the types of questions the examiner will ask about holidays. These might be quite general, such as the types of holidays that you enjoy, or they could be quite specific, such as a particular holiday that you remember from your childhood. Look at the dictionary results and write down those which you could incorporate into your answers. List them according to grammatical function. Examples might be:

- **Adjectives**
Dream holiday
Fun-filled holiday
Package holiday
Activity holiday

- Verbs
Have a holiday
Go on holiday
Take a holiday
Book a holiday

- Nouns
Holiday resort
Holiday season
Holiday cottage
Holiday romance

- Preposition
On holiday

- Phrases
Holiday of a lifetime

3. Learn and use the collocations

Think about all the possible IELTS holiday questions and prepare possible answers using the collocations. It's always a good idea to record yourself because when you play them back it will help fix them in your memory. The aim of this is not to memorise the whole answer, the examiner will notice and penalise you, but to memorise the collocations.

If you find yourself using adjectives, nouns, and verbs etc. which don't feature in the collocation dictionary then beware. It's possible that you are using language which is technically correct but sounds strange to a native speaker because it doesn't collocate. For example, we don't usually *buy* or *obtain* a holiday, nor do we have a *likeable* or *pleasing* holiday.

Idiomatic language

An idiom is a commonly used phrase or expression whose meaning is different from the literal meaning of its words. So, for example, you could tell the examiner that you were *over the moon* when you got your new job. This means that you were jubilant and delighted but if you hadn't heard this expression before it's unlikely that you would understand its meaning.

Idioms separate good users of English from the proficient ones and you will increase your band score if you use them correctly. The problem, however, is that if you get them slightly wrong, it's glaringly obvious and you will lose marks. You need to use the exact phrase and you need to get the context right. You can't say *on top of the moon* because it sounds ridiculous. Nor can you use it to describe something that was merely pleasurable; it has to be something you were very excited about. You can, incidentally, say *on top of the world*.

There is, alas, no easy way to learn idioms. There are dictionaries of idioms available but all the ones I have seen contain thousands, some of which are not in current everyday use. Many idioms are in informal usage only and informal language changes over time. Ideally, you need to write down the idioms you come across when reading English-language newspapers and watching English-language films. At that stage, you can use a dictionary or a Google search to obtain a detailed definition and to find other examples of its use. Only then, when you are absolutely sure of its meaning, should you use them in your exam. If in doubt, don't.

In the sample answers to common IELTS questions in the following chapters, I have incorporated many idioms in current usage. Appendix two, at the end of the book, has fifty, and also examples of how to incorporate them into part three of the test.

Paraphrase

The ability to paraphrase is an important skill to possess and I have noticed that it is often overlooked. It is important, not only because it is a band descriptor and the examiner will, therefore, be listening for examples of it, but also because, in some circumstances, it may provide a positive beginning for your answers. This is especially valuable in part two and we will look at this in more detail later.

Paraphrase means expressing something either written or spoken using different words, and there are three key ways of doing this; by changing key nouns and verbs for synonyms, by changing grammatical forms, and by changing tense structures.

• Using synonyms

Quite simply this means substituting words in the questions with others that have the same meaning. Here is a very simple example:

Examiner:
What do you like to do to relax?

Candidate:
At the end of a busy day, I like to unwind by ....

Here we have simply changed the verb *relax* to *unwind* which is a synonym having an almost exact meaning. Ideally, we should also replace the other verb in the question, *like*, as follows.

Candidate:
At the end of a busy day, I love to unwind by ....

• **Changing grammatical forms**

In the above example, I have replaced two keywords with synonyms. Ideally, you should also demonstrate that you can paraphrase by changing grammatical forms. In the following, the key verb in the question is changed to a noun:

Examiner:
What do you like to do to relax?

Candidate:
At the end of a busy day, relaxation is really important to me and I like to ...

You could also change the verb to an adjective:

At the end of a busy day, activities I find especially relaxing are:

• **Changing the tense structure**

In the relaxation question, the examiner uses the present simple and it is natural to answer in the same tense. If appropriate, you could use others:

At the end of a busy day I used to like to relax by ..., but I don't have time for that now so I ...

Next month yoga classes start at my college so I'm going to attend regularly which will hopefully help me to relax at the end of a busy day.

If I had the time, I would love to relax by ...

There are many more examples of paraphrasing in the sample answers for IELTS part two questions and it is when you are preparing for this part of the exam that you should particularly practice this skill. Please remember, however, that good paraphrasing skills need a good lexical resource and faultless grammar. It's more important to be accurate than to display a wide vocabulary. Don't take risks unless you are sure.

GRAMMATICAL RANGE AND ACCURACY

Here are the descriptors for grammatical range and accuracy at bands 7,8 and 9.

Band 7

• *uses a range of complex structures with some flexibility*

• *frequently produces error-free sentences, though some grammatical mistakes persist*

Band 8

• *uses a wide range of structures flexibly*

• *produces a majority of error-free sentences with only very occasional inappropriacies or basic/non-systematic errors*

Band 9

• *uses a full range of structures naturally and appropriately*

• *produces consistently accurate structures apart from 'slips 'characteristic of native speaker speech*

As you can see, these descriptors do not specify what grammar you should know and be able to use at any of the levels. However, the British Council does make a chart available that shows approximately how IELTS band scores map onto CEFR levels.

CEFR	B1			B2			C1			C2	
IELTS	4.0	4.5	5.0	5.5	6.0	6.5	7.0	7.5	8.0	8.5	9.0

In addition, we also know from the Common European Framework of Reference for Languages the types of grammatical structures in English you should be able to use without significant errors at each level. Since, for the purposes of this book, we are only interested in IELTS scores of 7.0 and above, we need to look closely at the grammar with which C1 and C2 users should be familiar. You should, of course, also be able to use the grammatical structures of the lower CEFR levels and I would recommend that you Google *CEFR grammar levels* so that you know what these are.

In this chapter, therefore, we will be looking closely at the grammatical structures which you are expected to know and be able to use at C1 and above. If you are able to incorporate these into your responses in an appropriate and natural way, as native speakers do, then you will be well on your way to a high band score. We will start with:

Phrasal Verbs

Phrasal verbs are possibly the biggest single indicator of proficiency in spoken English. Native speakers use them all the time whereas even near-fluent users of English as a second language often avoid them. And they are so easy to sidestep because there are always alternatives. Consider the following exchange:

Examiner
How much would you need to pay for a meal at a top restaurant in your city?

Candidate
Last time my family went for a celebratory meal my father paid over 50 euros for each of us.

This is a perfectly acceptable response but a grade 8 candidate, and a native speaker for that matter, might say the following:

Last time my family went for a celebratory meal my father had to fork out over 50 euros for each of us.

Not only will *fork out* gain you extra credit for grammatical range but it will also increase your score for lexical resource. This particular informal phrasal verb has a more nuanced meaning than *pay*. It indicates an element of unwillingness and, in the example above, suggests that the father was less than happy with the cost of the meal.

Unfortunately, for the student of English as a second language, phrasal verbs are made even more difficult by the fact that some, but not all, are able to be split. In other words, some phrasal verbs can have a noun placed in between the verb and the preposition. So, for example, you could say, *my girlfriend called off our date*, or *my girlfriend called our date off*.

Knowing which verbs may be split and which can't and being able to use the splittable forms in conversation is something which, according to the CEFR grammar framework, separates the C1 and C2 users from those who are merely at B2. Here is a basic outline of the four categories of phrasal verbs but I would recommend that you consult other resources. There are plenty available online. You just need to look them up!

Category 1 - Intransitive

These verbs do not have a direct object: e.g. break down

My car broke down last week and I had to take it to the garage to be repaired.

Category 2 - transitive and separable

These verbs need a direct object, and the preposition may be separated from the main verb

- if the object is a noun it may go before or after the preposition

- if the object is a pronoun then it must go before the preposition

e.g. drop off – *my colleague dropped off John at the railway station*, or - *my colleague dropped John off at the railway station.*

However, if we replace John with him then the sentence must be in this form - *my colleague dropped him off at the railway station.* You must not say, *my colleague dropped off him at the railway station.*

Category 3 - transitive and inseparable

These verbs need a direct object, but the preposition cannot be separated from the main verb

e.g. look after – *I'll look after your cat when you go on holiday*

You can't say - *I'll look your cat after when you go on holiday*

Category 4 - verbs with two prepositions:

e.g. *check up on - at work my boss is always checking up on me*

Please note these are also transitive and inseparable so you can't say, *my boss is always checking up me on*

There is an appendix at the end of this book that has a list of phrasal verbs which are particularly useful in the IELTS spoken test and also examples of how to incorporate them into sample answers.

Narrative tenses for experience

It is essential that you are able to use the full range of narrative tenses in order to achieve a good band score. And, as we shall see, they are particularly important in part two of the test. Hopefully, you are proficient in the use of the past simple, and it is possible to tell almost any story using this tense alone, but you will need to use the past simple in conjunction with the past continuous, past perfect simple, and past perfect continuous to give a more nuanced indication of the sequence of events. If you can use the narrative tenses with suitable linking words, then it will be easier to structure your part two talks.

As with phrasal verbs, there are plenty of online resources to help you with the narrative tenses but, as a brief overview, look at these two possible responses to a part two cue card:

> Describe an important decision you took a long time to make.
> You should say:
> what decision it was
> what difficulties you faced in making this decision
> how you made the decision
> and explain why it took you a long time to make this decision

1.

In my last year at school, I studied for exams and started to think about my future, in particular, what I was going to do at the age of eighteen. Basically, I had two choices, either get a job or go to university. One of my father's best friends is a man called Luigi. They were at school together and when they both left, Luigi started a small engineering company in our city. It became very successful. He and Dad remained friends and because I was always interested in machinery and technology, I often used to visit the factory when I was young. I even had a part-time job there during the school holidays when I was older.

When I worked for Luigi during the last of my school holidays, he offered me a full-time job as soon as my exams were over, and I was very tempted. But I also wanted to go to university. Most of my friends planned to go to university and I wanted to have that experience too.

It was a very difficult decision because I needed to get a student loan for my studies and be left with a big debt after three years. There was also no guarantee of a well-paid job just because I had a degree. To help make up my mind I sought advice from family and friends. My parents wanted me to get the job immediately after school. To them, it was a safe decision and they have never believed in borrowing money and having debt. But in the end, I spoke to the school teacher that I respected the most and then made my final decision. She implored me to go to university and so I did. I don't regret it.

2.

While I was studying for my exams in my last year at school I started to think about my future and, in particular, what I was going to do at the age of eighteen. Basically, I had two choices, either get a job or go to university. One of my father's best friends is a man called Luigi. They were at school together and having left, Luigi started a small engineering company in our city. It became very successful. He and Dad remained friends and because I was always interested in machinery and technology, I often used to visit the factory when I was young. I even had a part-time job there during the school holidays when I was older.

It was when I was working for Luigi during the last of my school holidays that he offered me a full-time job as soon as my exams were over. I was very tempted. But I also wanted to go to university. Most of my friends were planning to go to university and I wanted to have that experience too.

It was a very difficult decision because I would have needed to have got a student loan for my studies and be left with a big debt after three years. There was also no guarantee of a well-paid job just because I had a degree. While I was trying to make up my mind I sought advice from family and friends. My parents wanted me to get the job immediately after school. To them, it was a safe decision and they have never believed in borrowing money and having debt. But in the end, it was after I had spoken to the school teacher that I respected the most that I made my final decision. She implored me to go to university and so I did. I don't regret it.

The second will score more highly for grammatical range because, although it is essentially the same story as the first, it incorporates narrative tenses. These express with greater precision the sequence of events than the predominantly past simple tenses do in the first story.

In your practice sessions for part two try to incorporate at least one of the following narrative tense combinations:

• past continuous plus past simple to describe a longer background action being interrupted by a new event

> *It was while I was studying for my final exams at university that I realised I didn't want to be a lawyer after all.*

- past perfect plus past simple to describe something that happened before another action in the past.

> *It was after I had finished three years at law school that I told my parents I actually wanted to be a professional musician.*

- present perfect continuous plus past simple to describe a repeated or habitual action that takes place over an extended period of time followed by a single action.

> *After I have been running I always take a shower.*

> *I usually chill out and watch TV after I have been studying.*

Please note that in the above three sequences, you are able to change the tenses around without changing the meaning. For example:

past continuous plus past simple - *It was raining when I got up this morning.*

past simple plus past continuous - *When I got up this morning it was raining.*

Another way to indicate a sequence of events is to use a perfect participle followed by a past simple. The perfect participle indicates a completed action and you form it by putting *having* in front of a past participle. For example:

> *having spoken, having finished, having eaten, having paid, having watched, having arrived*

This is then followed by the past simple, as in the following examples:

> *Having paid the bill, we decided to leave the restaurant and go to the cinema.*

> *Having finished my studies for the day, I thought it was time for some fun.*

> *Having arrived at the airport, we had difficulty finding the check-in desk.*

Inversion with Negative Adverbials

You may read or be told that this grammatical construction is used primarily in written English and invariably in a formal context. In reality, native speakers do use it in normal everyday conversation. Rarely is it introduced to students of English as a second language until they reach advanced levels and, even then in my experience, often only briefly.

As a result, it is a construction not often used by non-native speakers. If you are able to incorporate it during your IELTS speaking test, and it only has to be once, then your examiner will definitely notice. And fortunately, they are incredibly easy to add since they are merely phrases used at the beginning of sentences to add emphasis. You just need to remember to invert the subject and the verb after the negative adverbial.

There is plenty of help online if you are unsure of the construction but here are ten of the most useful phrases. In addition, each phrase has been incorporated into a sample response to a question from former IELTS part one speaking tests.

- **Only then** ...

  Examiner
  What's your daily routine on a working day?

  Candidate
  I suppose like most people I shower and have breakfast but what I always try to do is at least twenty minutes of exercise and meditation. Only then do I leave the flat for work.

- **Never before** ...

  Examiner
  Which was your favourite holiday destination?

  Candidate
  Two years ago I went with some friends to the Greek Island of Kefalonia. It was just after our exams and we went there primarily to relax. It was ideal because there wasn't much to do apart from sitting in the sun all day and swimming. And our hotel was near to a famously idyllic beach called Myrtos. Never before have I seen such a beautiful coastline.

- **Rarely** ...

  Examiner
  What do you enjoy doing in your free time?

  Candidate
  At the end of a busy day, I try to visit the gym. I do genuinely enjoy it and because I sit at a desk all day I think it's important that I get some vigorous exercise as often as possible. Rarely do I manage it every day of the working week because of other commitments but I usually fit in three or four visits from Monday to Friday.

- **Seldom ...**

  ### Examiner
  What are the advantages of watching television instead of going to the cinema?

  ### Candidate
  Apart from cost, because an evening at the cinema is quite expensive, for me one of the biggest advantages of watching television is flexibility. These days you can pretty much watch what you want when you want. Seldom do I have the time to travel to my nearest multiplex.

- **Only later ...**

  ### Examiner
  Did you ever visit a zoo when you were a child?

  ### Candidate
  I loved going to zoos when I was really young and there was one in the city where I grew up, so we went as a family quite often. At the time I thought it was a great place because the cages were quite small, and you could get really close to the animals. Only later did I realise that from a welfare point of view, the animals were kept in wholly inadequate surroundings.

- **Not until ...**

  ### Examiner
  Has your preference in music ever changed

  ### Candidate
  When I was young I used to really dislike classical music. I thought it was boring and couldn't understand how people could sit through a whole symphony. Not until I started to learn how to play the piano did I come to appreciate how intricate and beautiful some classical music can be.

- **Not since ...**

  ### Examiner
  Do you like rainy days?

  ### Candidate
  Not since childhood have I enjoyed rainy days. Then I really didn't care what the weather was like. I didn't worry about having to be in certain places at particular times. Now I just find the rain inconvenient. For one thing, the traffic in my city seems to grind to a halt.

- **No sooner ...**

    Examiner
    How did you get here today?

    Candidate
    I came by public transport and fortunately everything went according to plan. No sooner had I arrived at the station this morning than the train came.

- **On no account**

    Examiner
    Do you think it is important to learn about history?

    Candidate
    I think that it is crucial to have an understanding of the past if we are to avoid making the same mistakes in the future. So, on no account should we stop learning about history.

- **Under no circumstances ...**

    Examiner
    Do you have a pet?

    Candidate
    Unfortunately not because I absolutely adore animals and there was always a dog at home when I was growing up. I would love to have one now, but I live in a flat. Under no circumstances would I consider owning a dog until I had a house with a garden.

Mixed conditionals

You should hopefully be familiar with, and be able to use, first, second, and third conditionals and it will increase your band score if you incorporate them into the test. Try, if possible, to also include mixed conditionals into your conversation with the examiner. You won't always find a suitable opportunity for their use but there are a number of examples in the sample answers in the following chapters.

As for the grammar, it is possible for the two parts of a conditional sentence to refer to different times, and the resulting sentence is referred to as a mixed conditional. There are two main categories:

1. Present result of a past condition.

In this category, the tense in the if clause is the past perfect, and the tense in the main clause is the present conditional. Don't forget that, as in all conditional sentences, the order of the clauses is not fixed. You may have to rearrange the pronouns when you change the order of the clauses, but the meaning is exactly the same. This category of mixed conditional refers to an unreal past condition and its probable result in the present.

Let's look at some examples we can use in the exam in response to questions from the examiner.

Examiner
Do you think children should play less sport at school and spend more time in the classroom?

Candidate
In the long term, I think you are likely to get a much better job as a result of studying for long hours when you are younger. For example, if I had spent more time in the library than on the football pitch I would probably earn more money now.

Examiner
Do you want to change your current job?

Candidate
I think about it sometimes but it's probably too late now. I would undoubtedly be with another company if I had been more decisive a few years ago.

Examiner
Do you prefer to live in the centre of town or in the country?

Candidate
I live in the town because it is more convenient for work, but in many respects, I wish I lived in the country. If I had known how noisy and dirty the town can be, I would be renting a cottage in a village now.

2. Past result of present or continuing condition.

In this second category of a mixed-conditional sentence, the tense in the if clause is the simple past, and the tense in the main clause is the perfect conditional. These mixed conditional sentences refer to an unreal present situation and its likely, but still unreal past result. In these mixed conditional sentences, the time in the if clause is now, and the time in the main clause is in the past. Hopefully, this will be clearer from the examples below.

Examiner
Do you think people should use public transport more?

Candidate
I very much agree that people should, and I really wish that they did in my city. If public transport was more efficient and people stopped using cars, the quality of life for everybody would have improved.

Examiner
Which do you prefer: eating in restaurants or eating at home?

Candidate
Definitely the former because I'm not a particularly talented cook. If I knew how to prepare good food at home, I wouldn't have spent so much money eating out over the years.

Examiner
What problems are there with shopping in your town?

Candidate
Generally, the town centre is very good for shopping and there is a wide range of shops. Parking can be a problem though. If more space was available for cars in the centre people wouldn't have started to use online retail in such a big way.

Implied conditions

It's useful to remember that the if clause may be implied rather than stated so we often don't actually need to use the word *if*. Conditional verbs are, however, still used in the result clause. This type of construction sounds very natural to native speakers and can be very useful in all parts of the speaking test. Here are some examples:

I would love to try to get a new job, but I don't think I stand a chance.

I would have enjoyed playing more sport at school, but my parents wanted me to study all the time.

I enjoy travelling. I would have gone to America last year, but I didn't have enough money.

Most students have to borrow money in my country, otherwise they wouldn't be able to go to college.

My grandmother tries to get out and see her friends every day, otherwise I think she would be quite lonely.

The public transport is cheap and efficient, otherwise I would have to buy a car for my daily commute to work.

PRONUNCIATION

Many of my IELTS students have worried unnecessarily about pronunciation and the main reason is that they have confused pronunciation with accent. All native English speakers have some sort of accent and there is a huge variety of them. I was born and brought up in Nottingham, which is in the middle of England, and I use different vowel sounds from a person from the south of the country. However, we have absolutely no problems understanding each other. You, when you are speaking English as a second language, will inevitably have an accent and it is because of the unavoidable influence of your mother tongue.

But this does not matter and, as long as your accent does not impede understanding, you need not be concerned. Whatever you do, don't try to change your accent, instead focus on such pronunciation features as stress and intonation because how you use these will determine your band score.

Pronunciation band descriptors

Band 7

• *shows all the positive features of Band 6 and some, but not all, of the positive features of Band 8*

Band 8

• *uses a wide range of pronunciation features*

• *sustains flexible use of features, with only occasional lapses*

• *is easy to understand throughout; L1 accent has minimal effect on intelligibility*

Band 9

• *uses a full range of pronunciation features with precision and subtlety*

• *sustains flexible use of features throughout*

• *is effortless to understand*

We will ignore the descriptor for band 7 because it is not very helpful for our purposes and instead look at those for 8 and 9. In particular, note that to achieve a score of 8 your accent should have only a minor effect on your intelligibility and, at band 9, not at all. As long as the examiner can understand you, then your accent is irrelevant and, indeed, he or she will expect you to have one. What the examiner will be listening for is how you use the key pronunciation features.

Pronunciation features

1. Individual sounds

There are 24 consonant and 20 vowel sounds in English and it's entirely possible that some of these don't exist in your native tongue. What you are first going to need to do is identify which, if any, you have difficulties with. Ideally, you will have access to a native English speaker or English teacher who will be able to tell you, but there are also many resources online. If, for example, you Google *English pronunciation problems for Spanish speakers*, you will find a large number of resources that will tell you, among other things, that Spanish has far fewer vowel sounds than English. Exchange *Spanish* for your own native language and you will discover what particular difficulties you might face.

Second, you are going to need to model these sounds. In other words, you will need to hear how native English speakers make them. One possibility is to use an online dictionary that has audio. There are a number of these, but Macmillan is possibly the best. Another is to use a phonemic chart. There are interactive versions online and you can also download them as apps for your mobile device. The creator of the chart is a teacher called Adrian Underhill and he has a number of excellent online resources and videos to help you master the sounds of the English language.

When you have modelled the sounds you will then need to practice them. Repeat them over and over and ideally record yourself. Try putting the sounds into words and then sentences.

2. Syllable stress

Individual words are made up of syllables and, if there are two or more, one of them will be stressed more heavily than the others. It's crucial to get this right because if you don't, you simply won't be understood. What complicates the situation further is that a few English words change their meaning according to where the stress is placed. This usually happens when the word can function as both a noun and a verb. *Present* and *produce* are two common examples but there are many others.

The basic rules are as follows:

Two-syllable nouns and adjectives	stress on the first syllable
Two-syllable verbs	stress is on the second syllable
Two-syllable words which are both a noun and a verb	following on from the rules above, the noun is stressed on the first and the verb is stressed on the last syllable
Three syllable words ending in *ly* and *er* such as *silently* and *easier*	stress is on the first syllable
Words ending with *tion*, *sion*, and *ic* such as *desperation*, *confusion*, and *archaic*	stress is on the second-to-last syllable
Words ending in *al*, *cy*, *ty*, *gy*, and *phy* such as *multifunctional*, *proficiency*, *respectability*, *technology*, *autobiography*	stress is on the third-to-last syllable
Compound nouns - these are words formed from two nouns such as *football*, *fireworks*, and *blackboard*	stress is on the first noun
Compound adjectives - these often have hyphens as in *part-time* and *free-range*	stress is on the second word

It is beyond the scope of this book to detail all the rules, and their exceptions, which can help you determine word stress in English but if you have any doubts there are many free resources online. Please remember also that, although these rules may seem complicated, most native speakers don't know them. They automatically place the stress in the right place and by listening and practising you will too.

3. Sentence stress

Languages are either syllable-timed or stress-timed. In a syllable-timed language, all the syllables will tend to follow each other at regular intervals and an equal amount of time will be given to each. Italian, Spanish, Mandarin, Cantonese, Brazilian Portuguese, and Turkish are some examples of syllable-timed languages. In these languages the more syllables there are in the sentence, the longer it will take to say it.

In stress-timed languages, however, not all syllables are given the same amount of time. Instead, the words which carry the meaning, such as the verbs, nouns, and adjectives are stressed while the grammatical words, the words which give the sentence structure, such as the articles and propositions are not. English, European Portuguese, Russian, and Arabic are examples of stress-timed languages.

One result of English being a stress-timed language is that those unstressed words are said very quickly, they have to be squashed up to fit the rhythm. I've heard some students describe it as if the words are almost 'swallowed.'

Let's look at an example of a short sentence where the structure words have been removed leaving just the meaning words.

...... buy .... cat .... scare ...... mice

It should be easy to understand the sentence even though some of it is missing. The reason is that these four words, two nouns and two verbs, carry the meaning. These are the words that will be stressed.

Here's the complete sentence with the structure words included.

*I will **buy** a **cat** in order to **scare** the **mice.***

Now imagine saying this sentence to the beat of a metronome, the device used by musicians to mark time. The four stressed words, those meaning words in bold, must match the tick of the metronome. What you should immediately notice is that you have one syllable between ***buy*** and ***cat*** but four syllables between ***cat*** and ***scare.*** Those four are going to have to be squashed together and said very quickly. It will sound something like *norderta* which would make no sense if said on its own.

It's this squashing together of unstressed syllables that gives spoken English its rhythm. It also, incidentally, makes listening to spoken English particularly difficult for those learning the language.

The following tables will help you know which are meaning words and which are structure words:

Meaning words - stressed	Example
main verbs	*buy, eat, give*
nouns	*cat, John, tree*
adjectives	*small, blue, beautiful*
adverbs	*always, slowly, often*
negative auxiliaries	*won't, hasn't, can't*

Structure words - unstressed	Example
pronouns	*he, we, they*
prepositions	*on, at, into*
articles	*a, an, the*
conjunctions	*and, but, because*
auxiliary verbs	*do, be, have, can, must*

4. Shifting stress

As if this wasn't complicated enough, we can sometimes change or shift the stress pattern in order to modify the meaning. Look at this sentence:

I don't think it will rain tomorrow.

Usually, we wouldn't stress the first word, *I*, because it is a pronoun. The first stress in the sentence would be *don't*, the negative auxiliary. However, you can shift the stress from *don't* to *I* in order to modify the meaning. If this happens, what the speaker is actually implying is this:

Everybody thinks it will be wet tomorrow, but, personally, I don't think it will rain.

To achieve a band score of 7.0 or above in the pronunciation section the examiner will want to hear that you are able to use correct word stress in order to emphasise or focus your meaning. Let's, therefore, look at another short sentence and consider how changing the stress on individual words can change the meaning.

She *said that speaking English is easy.*

she in particular and not somebody else

She said that **speaking** *English is easy.*

whereas writing and listening are difficult

She said that speaking **English** *is easy.*

whereas speaking other languages is difficult.

5. Weak sounds

Something you may already know is that the most common sound in English is what is called the *schwa*. The phonemic symbol is ə

It is the short, always unstressed, vowel sound that native speakers make for the second syllable of the word *weather* and it accounts for about a third of all vowel sounds that native speakers make. It can be spelt with any of the vowel letters and it occurs in a huge number of words many of which are the grammatical structure words described above. It also forms the unstressed syllable of many meaning words.

What you do need to be aware of, however, and your examiner will be listening for this, is that a number of words can have both a strong pronunciation and a weak schwa sound depending on their importance in the sentence.

Take the word *do* for example. It can either have a strongly pronounced long oo sound or it can have the short schwa.

Look at this sentence:

What do you want to do at the weekend?

The first *do* has a short unstressed schwa vowel sound because it is an auxiliary and a structure word. The second *do*, however, is a main verb, a meaning word, and so it will be stressed with the longer oo sound.

Note, however, that a number of structure words can also have both the weak and strong pronunciations.

Look at this sentence:

Lucy can speak English very well.

If the speaker is making a simple statement about Lucy, then *can* will be unstressed, and the vowel sound will be the weak schwa sound.

If, however, a friend of the speaker said, *I don't think Lucy can speak English*, and the speaker knew that this wasn't true, the response might be:

*She **can**, and she speaks it very well indeed.*

In this sentence, the *can* will be stressed, and it will have a different vowel sound. It will be the same vowel sound as the first syllable in **ap**ple.

The pronunciation of the schwa quickly signals whenever you are merely a good speaker of English or whenever you are a fluent one and your examiner will know from the very first few words that you speak which category you are in. The best way to practice is to record a native speaker on a news or weather programme and write down a few sentences marking the weak schwa sounds. It will look something like this:

A good deal of cloud around today, and we could see some rain at times, especially in the west. However, if there are any cloud breaks further east, it will be very warm for the time of year.

By marking the schwa sounds you will become aware of just how common they are. Repeat the sentences over and over until your sounds match those of the original recording.

6. Intonation

Intonation is a feature of pronunciation common to all languages. It's about how we say something rather than what we say, and it's sometimes called the music of speech. A change in the pitch, whether the words rise or fall, may change the meaning of those words.

I've also sometimes heard the function of intonation described as being like body language. You can invariably tell when you are talking to someone whether they are bored or interested in what you are saying from such things as their posture, the inclination of their head, and where their eyes are moving.

You, when you are speaking, can express a huge range of attitudes such as boredom, interest, annoyance, and happiness simply from your intonation. Native British English speakers are particularly good at using intonation to convey sarcasm and irony.

Consider the following exchange:

John
I'm going to get up at five tomorrow morning to go for a run before I head off for work.

Lucy
Yes, I'm sure you will.

By changing her intonation Lucy can signal that she totally believes that John will do this, or that she thinks it a little unlikely, or even that it's one of the most stupid things she's heard him say.

There are a number of ways that the pitch of our voices can change - a simple rise or fall, or a more complex fall followed by a rise, or the opposite, a rise followed by a fall. What you can also do is maintain a flat intonation with neither a rise nor a fall. This is what native speakers do to convey a neutral attitude and it's also what they do when they are bored.

Non-native speakers also tend to maintain a flat intonation because they are thinking too much about what they are saying rather than how they are saying it. In the IELTS exam, you are going to be asked about things that you like, and you really don't want to signal to the examiner that you aren't actually interested in anything. Typically, to show enthusiasm when we are speaking about a subject our voices rise towards the middle of sentences and then fall at the end.

To improve your own intonation you first need to become aware of the patterns that native speakers use. The type of programmes that we might watch to improve our pronunciation, such as news and documentaries, are okay but ideally, we need to listen to actors displaying a range of emotions. Movies are obviously a good choice for this but so are situation comedies. Listen to segments carefully but without paying attention to what is being said. Instead be conscious of the changes in pitch, the natural rising and falling, of the actors' voices.

When you feel that you are fully aware of the intonation patterns try to copy them. Record yourself and compare it with the original. Also, choose one of the sample part two answers in this book and record yourself speaking it. Then place yourself in the position of an examiner listening to you. Do you sound bored or do you sound enthusiastic and interested in what you are talking about?

7. Chunking

To achieve a score of 7.0 or more in the pronunciation section you will need to display to the examiner that you are able to chunk certain groups of words when you speak.

Consider the following exchange:

John
How are you?

Lucy
Not so bad thanks.

In neither John's question nor in Lucy's response will the words usually be pronounced individually with gaps in-between. Instead, the words will be squashed together to form one chunk. It's because this is a standard exchange that two people who know each other will make when meeting. John is not asking for specific information that Lucy needs to pay special attention to and she is not saying anything she hasn't said, or that he has heard, on numerous previous occasions.

This type of word chunking is not limited to standard polite greetings. Native speakers squash together many phrases when they are speaking, and you will need to do this when you are talking to the examiner.

As a general rule, the words that are chunked are the connecting phrases in your speech. These are the little groups of words that people use all the time and don't actually mean very much on their own. The linking devices containing more than one word, for example, *as a result*, are all examples of these, but so are virtually all of the common phrases that we use in everyday speech. The listener has heard them before, they don't carry any message and should, therefore, be pronounced as one fluid sound without any noticeable gaps.

Here are some examples:

As I've already said ...
On the other hand ...
I'm not really sure but ...
It could be because ...
I've been told that ...
Maybe it's because ...
In my opinion ...

Again, as with all of these sections on IELTS pronunciation, you will only improve your own ability to chunk phrases by first making sure that you are aware of others doing it and then copying. Make listening to English language radio news programmes and podcasts, watching TED Talks, YouTube videos, and movies part of your daily routine. And, above all, practice as often as you can. Listening and copying is the key to having the pronunciation of a native speaker and a high IELTS band score.

PART ONE

The inform and qualify strategy

The first part of the speaking test will last for about four to five minutes and it is generally considered to be the easiest. The main reason for this is because many of the questions will be about you. You should already know the answers and you can prepare for many in advance. One possible problem with part one, however, is that the questions are too easy, and you are tempted to respond with answers that are too short and lacking the essential vocabulary and grammar which will give you a high band score. We will look at how to avoid this by first considering the difference between closed and open questions.

Look at these two sets of three common IELTS questions:

What job do you do?

When do you usually get up in the morning?

Do you spend much time with your family?

What kinds of people are most likely to be successful in their work?

Do you think it is possible to learn time management skills?

How do you think the family will change in the future?

The first three are typical questions from part one of the exam and are examples of closed questions. These are questions that can be answered with a single word or a short sentence. So possible responses to the first three questions are these:

I'm a waiter

At seven

Yes

The second three are open questions and are from part three. You can't respond with one word or sentence, instead, you have to provide a much longer answer. You are being asked about your opinions and feelings and you will need to think and reflect.

Many part one questions are of the closed type and you could potentially respond quickly with one or two words. However, you must resist the temptation to do this. The key is to provide the information requested and then qualify it. By *qualify*, I mean that you add an extra fact or two which makes the statement less absolute.

You will also need to use a wide vocabulary resource, idiomatic language, and a range of grammatical structures. It's unlikely, but not impossible, that you are going to have the opportunity to such complex structures as mixed conditionals or the tense sequences described in the grammatical range chapter - these are more for parts two and three of the test - but you should consider what idioms, phrasal verbs and less common vocabulary you can incorporate.

And finally, make sure that your responses are not too long. Two or three short sentences are enough. In the first sentence, you should provide the information requested and then follow this up with an additional detail or two which qualifies this information in some way.

Here are sample responses from those first three part one questions:

Examiner
What job do you do?

Candidate
I'm a waiter. It's not a long-term career though, just a means to an end. Hopefully, by this time next year, I will have saved up enough to do a full-time degree course.

Examiner
When do you usually get up in the morning?

Candidate
Usually at seven. This is on a weekday though because I need to be at work by nine. At the weekend I can take it easy and lie in until mid-morning.

Examiner
Do you spend much time with your family?

Candidate
I would if I could. Unfortunately, only during the holidays do I get the chance to visit because they live so far away.

In each of these three responses I have directly answered the question in the first sentence but then, in my second sentence or two, I have qualified this response. In addition, the answers are short and succinct, and they also incorporate some of the vocabulary and grammatical devices which will help you achieve a high band score.

These are:

• *Means to an end* - an idiom meaning something that is not important in itself but is useful in achieving an aim.

• *I will have saved up* - here I have used the future perfect tense in combination with a phrasal verb. To save up means to keep money aside so that you can use it for a special reason in the future.

• *Take it easy* - this is an idiom meaning to rest, relax or be calm.

• *Lie in* - this is a phrasal verb meaning to remain in bed after the usual time that you would get up.

• *I would if I could* - a very useful and pithy conditional phrase.

• *Only during the holidays do I* - a negative adverbial construction.

Topics and questions

Let's now look in more detail at the structure of part one and a list of the possible topics, questions, and sample answers.

It is likely that the examiner will start part one of the test by asking questions from one or two of the following four topics - work, study, hometown, and home. Work and study are usually mutually exclusive, in other words, most people do either one or the other. There are exceptions to this of course but the examiner will invariably ask you about one of these two depending on which is relevant to you. He or she will actually know in advance which is more appropriate because you will have specified what you do on your IELTS application form. However, he or she may still ask a question in the following format:

   Do you work or study?

Here are some possible responses based on the inform and qualify system detailed above:

I'm currently working. It's a fairly run-of-the-mill nine-to-five job in an insurance office. Essentially, it's a stopgap until I can find employment in my specialist field which is cybersecurity.

I'm studying physics at university and I'm three quarters through a four-year course. It's been tough, but the end is in sight and I'm looking forward to moving on to full-time work.

Actually, I do both because I'm studying law at college and working part-time in a supermarket. If I didn't have to do the latter, I wouldn't but unfortunately, my course costs a fortune.

Notes:

• *Run-of-the-mill* - this is an idiomatic expression that indicates that something is ordinary and not particularly interesting or exciting.

• *Nine-to-five job* - is one with predictable hours, usually an office. It has a slightly negative connotation.

• *Stopgap* - this is something that serves a purpose for a short time until something better or more suitable is found.

• *The end is in sight* - a useful phrase indicating that the conclusion to something will happen soon.

• *Look forward* - a very common phrasal verb that you should know and be able to use. It means that you are pleased and excited by something that is going to happen in the future.

• *Move on* - a phrasal verb meaning to start something new.

• *If I didn't have to ..., I wouldn't* - this is a handy conditional you can use to describe anything you are obliged to do but would prefer not to.

• *Costs a fortune* - an idiomatic phrase meaning that something is extremely expensive.

Instead of asking whether you work or study, the examiner may lead directly into questions about one or the other depending on which your application form has indicated is more appropriate. The examiner will typically ask a couple of questions from one of these topics. Here are some possible questions with sample responses:

Work

Examiner

What is your job?

Candidate

I'm an accountant. I've only recently qualified and in my first year with my company so I'm on the bottom rung of a very long career ladder.

Examiner

Do you enjoy your job?

Candidate

Very much so. People joke about accountants being boring bean counters, but accountancy is certainly not dull. The work that we do for companies can mean the difference between them thriving or underperforming.

Examiner

Why did you decide to do that job?

Candidate

It wasn't an easy decision. I weighed up all the pros and cons but what attracted me was the stability and long-term career prospects. People will always need accountants.

Examiner

Do you get on well with your colleagues?

Candidate

I do. I'm in a small close-knit team and although we are quite competitive we have the same values and aspirations. We move in the same circles and so we often socialise at weekends.

Examiner

Do you plan to continue with your job in the long term?

Candidate

Definitely. I'm in it for the long haul. Promotion, I hope, is just around the corner and the prospects for a lasting and lucrative career are promising.

Notes:

• *On the bottom rung of the ladder* - at the lowest level in a company in terms of pay and status.

• *A bean counter* - someone who obsessively examines expenditure with a view to saving money. It is a common disparaging term for an accountant.

• *To weigh up* - a phrasal verb meaning to consider the advantages and disadvantages of something before making a decision. It is often used as part of the idiomatic phrase - *to weigh up the pros and cons.*

• *Close-knit* - an idiom used to describe people bound together by common interests and strong relationships.

• *Move in the same circles* - when people move in the same circles they socialise with others who have the same interests and lifestyle.

• *In it for the long haul* - indicates an intention to do something for a long time, perhaps permanently.

• *Just around the corner* - an idiom meaning that something is likely to happen in the near future. It can, of course, be used literally as in, there is a restaurant just around the corner.

Study

Examiner
What are you studying?

Candidate
I'm studying modern languages. English and German are my two principal areas of learning with Mandarin as my minor course.

Examiner
Why did you choose to study that subject?

Candidate

It's principally because I had a flair for languages when I was at school. I assumed that I would enjoy the subject at university. It's also considered to be a stepping stone to a diversity of fulfilling careers.

Examiner

Is it a popular subject to study?

Candidate

Modern language courses are massively oversubscribed in my country. They seem to be all the rage. I'm sure it's because good linguists are highly sought after in the global jobs market.

Examiner

What do you enjoy most about your studies?

Candidate

Above all, it's the opportunity to connect with other cultures. I truly believe that language and culture go hand in glove and that it's only when you speak somebody else's language that you can truly understand their art, music, and literature.

Examiner

What do you hope to do when you have finished studying?

Candidate

My aim is to have a year abroad. If all goes according to plan my university will help me get a work placement with a German company. With luck and hard work that could open doors to a permanent job there.

Notes:

• *To have a flair for* something means that you have a special talent or aptitude for that thing.

• *Stepping stone* - this is an opportunity that leads to better things.

• *All the rage* - an idiom meaning something that is currently very fashionable or popular. It wasn't in the past and might not be in the future, but it is now.

• *Sought after* - if something is *sought after* it is rare or much in demand.

• *Hand in glove* - an idiom meaning in a close relationship or association.

• *Goes according to plan* - this is a phrase that means that something happens in exactly the way that it was intended to happen.

• *To open doors* - if something or someone opens doors it means that they create an opportunity or make something possible.

After work and study, the questions most likely to be asked will be about your hometown and your home. By hometown, the examiner means the place where you were born and spent your early years. It's likely to be the place where you went to school. This might not necessarily be the place where you are living now.

Your home, on the other hand, is the actual building - the house, apartment, flat, or student accommodation where you are currently residing.

Hometown

Examiner
Where is your hometown?

Candidate
My hometown is a place called Queluz. It's a medium-sized town some twenty kilometres to the north-west of Lisbon. It's effectively a dormitory suburb of the capital.

Examiner
What do you like about it?

Candidate
It's compact and fairly self-contained. Although it's close to a big city you don't actually need to go there. Everything you need on a day-to-day basis is close at hand such as a wide range of shops, bars, and restaurants.

Examiner

Do you visit often?

Candidate

I don't unfortunately. Now that I'm studying abroad it's prohibitively expensive to go back often. And I am constrained by time. I'm afraid that it is a case of high days and holidays.

Examiner

Has it changed much since you were young?

Candidate

Well, yes and no. It doesn't actually look very different but there has been a demographic transformation that might not be immediately obvious. Essentially what's happened is that lots of younger people, like me, have moved away in search of opportunities elsewhere.

Examiner

Is there much for a tourist to see in your hometown?

Candidate

Oh, for certain. On the edge of the town is an exquisite eighteenth-century former royal palace which is open to the public. It's surrounded by splendid formal gardens. If you ever get the chance I would definitely recommend that you visit.

Notes:

• *A dormitory suburb* - this is a place from which people travel in order to work in a nearby bigger town or city.

• *Self-contained* - if something is self-contained it has everything that is needed within itself. Many things may be self-contained - towns, flats, or even people.

• *Day-to-day* - something that happens every day as a regular part of your job or life.

• *Close at hand* - an idiom meaning nearby.

• *Prohibitively expensive* - a collocation and a much better way of saying *very expensive*.

• *Constrained by time* - a more interesting way of saying that you don't have enough time.

• *High days and holidays* - an idiom meaning special occasions.

• *Demographic transformation* - a way of saying that the age distribution in a place has changed. It can be caused by younger people moving away or by a change to lower birth and death rates in a community.

• *Not immediately obvious* - a collocation indicating that something is unlikely to be noticed at once. You can also use *not immediately apparent*.

• *Exquisite* - a better alternative to *very beautiful*.

• *If you ever get the chance I would definitely recommend that ...* - there should be at least one opportunity to use this conditional phrase during your IELTS test.

Home

Examiner
Do you live in an apartment or a house?

Candidate
I live in a small self-contained apartment on the fifth floor of a tower block. The location is not ideal, but it's fit for purpose and cheap and cheerful.

Examiner
Who do you live with?

Candidate
I live on my own in splendid solitude. Well, that's not strictly accurate - I share my flat with a cat. He adopted me, and I had no choice in the matter.

Examiner
What do you like most about your home?

Candidate
It's incredibly quiet. Most of my neighbours are older retired people who are not exactly party animals. This suits me down to the ground as I spend most of my evenings studying.

Examiner

What would you change about your home if you could?

Candidate

I would move it lock, stock, and barrel five kilometres in a south-westerly direction. It's a great apartment but it's in the middle of nowhere.

Examiner

Do you plan to stay there for a long time?

Candidate

Staying there is a means to an end. It's cheap enough to live there while I'm studying but one day, hopefully in the not-too-distant future, I'll move closer to the centre of the city.

Notes:

• *Fit for purpose* - an idiom meaning that something is good enough for what it is supposed to do.

• *Cheap and cheerful* - one of my favourite idioms meaning that something is inexpensive but pleasant and of good enough quality.

• *Splendid solitude* - a collocation to describe somebody who enjoys being alone.

• *Have no choice in the matter* - a phrase used to describe a situation where there is no alternative.

(My answer to this question, incidentally, is one where I have used a touch of whimsical humour. You certainly shouldn't set out to entertain or amuse the examiner but, if you can make him or her smile once, it won't do any harm.)

• *A party animal* - an idiom used to describe an extrovert person who enjoys parties and lively social events.

• *Suits me down to the ground* - a useful idiom. If something suits you down to the ground, it suits you perfectly.

• *Lock, stock, and barrel* - a phrase meaning absolutely everything.

• *Middle of nowhere* - this is an idiom used to describe a building or place that is isolated or in an inconvenient location.

• *A means to an end* - something that is not valued or important in itself but is useful in achieving a particular aim.

• *In the not-too-distant future* - an idiom meaning soon.

You can almost guarantee that you will be asked questions about one, or possibly two, of these four topics - work, study, hometown, home - in part one of the exam. You will also be asked about an additional topic. It is impossible to predict in advance what this topic will be because they change all the time. I call these the wildcard topics because they can sometimes seem to be quite random. However, they are what most candidates would describe as 'easy' subjects.

You are not going to be asked about anything way beyond your comfort zone such as quantum physics or seventeenth-century opera. Nor will you be quizzed about anything contentious or controversial such as politics or religion. Instead, they will be relatively gentle questions about such things as sport, leisure, and travel. Many will be in the form of, *Do you like ...?* or *What do you think of ...?*

And just as in the work and home topics many of the questions will be closed. But, just as before, don't be tempted to give answers which are too brief. Use the inform and qualify system and provide two or three sentences.

Here are five classic part one wildcard topics with typical questions and possible answers.

Leisure

Examiner
What do you enjoy doing in your free time?

Candidate
Ideally, I like to meet up with friends either in a cafe or a restaurant. At this time of year, you can sit outside at one of the street cafes and it's great to while away an hour or two relaxing and catching up with old friends.

Examiner
How much time do you have for this?

Candidate

Well to be honest, not as much as I would like. When we were all young, carefree, and single we could spend every night out on the town. These days, alas, such evenings are few and far between. But, I suppose, I appreciate them all the more.

Examiner

What are common leisure activities in your country?

Candidate

Spending the evening at home seems to be increasingly popular. A combination of services like Netflix, high-definition streaming, and hundreds of niche YouTube channels means that you don't need to venture out for entertainment. I think it's turning us into a nation of couch potatoes.

Notes:

• *Meet up with* - the phrasal verb to meet up is slightly more nuanced than the simple to meet on its own. It implies something planned and for a purpose.

• *While away* - a phrasal verb meaning to spend time in a relaxed and pleasant way.

• *Catch up with* - this phrasal verb can have several meanings but when it is used in connection with friends and family it means that you meet in order to update each other on what has been happening since the last time you saw each other.

• *Out on the town* - if you spend an evening out on the town it means that you are enjoying the places of entertainment such as bars and nightclubs.

• *Few and far between* - an idiom meaning infrequently.

• *couch potatoes* – an idiom meaning people who take very little exercise and spend lots of time watching television.

Food

Examiner
What is your favourite food?

Candidate
Oh, it's definitely pizza. I sort of wish it wasn't and I would much prefer telling you that my dish of choice is a tofu and quinoa salad. Unfortunately, however, a pizza loaded with every unhealthy topping possible is my go-to comfort food.

Examiner
Have your favourite foods changed since you were a child?

Candidate
Yes and no. Lots of things that I relished as a child, like pizza and chips and chocolate, I still do. But my tastes have changed and there are things that I appreciate now that I thought were revolting when I was young. Olives and anchovies spring to mind. I can't get enough of them now.

Examiner
Do you eat healthily?

Candidate
Well, sort of. I genuinely do try, and I make a concerted effort to consume the recommended quantities of fruits and vegetables. I'm also cutting down on red meats and processed foods. But unfortunately, I sometimes can't resist temptation, especially when I am in a restaurant and there is pizza on the menu.

Notes:

• *Go-to* - used as an adjective *go-to* means the first person or item you choose in a particular situation without giving the matter much thought.

• *Comfort food* - this is an idiom denoting food that has some nostalgic or sentimental appeal. It is often a food that a person enjoyed in childhood and it is invariably heavy in either carbohydrates or sugar.

• *To relish* - is a good verb to use to describe something that you like very much. It is particularly associated with the enjoyment of food.

- *Spring to mind* - an idiom meaning that you suddenly remember or think of something.

- *Can't get enough* (of something) - an idiomatic way of saying that you like something very much.

- *Make a concerted effort* - this is a collocation meaning that you try very hard to do something.

- *Cut down on* (something) - a phrasal verb meaning to eat or drink less of something, usually for health reasons.

Sport

Examiner
Do you play any sports?

Candidate
If only! I really wish that I had the time but at the moment I have too many commitments. I used to play tennis regularly until studying and exams got in the way. Just now I have to content myself with being an armchair sportsman.

Examiner
What are the most popular sports in your country?

Candidate
The most popular has to be football and it's more akin to a religion than a sport to some people. But unless you are a young male it's primarily a spectator sport. For competitive physical activities that lots of people actually participate in as opposed to just watching on TV, basketball, and volleyball are enjoyed by both sexes of all ages.

Examiner
Should children be required to play sports at school?

Candidate
Yes, but with some reservations. Children should certainly be encouraged to be active for health reasons but not all enjoy or are good at competitive team sports. If a wider variety of physical activities were on offer at schools, such as mountain biking or orienteering,

then I think kids would be more likely to continue them when they become adults.

Notes:

• *If only!* - A great expression which in just two words means: *What you have said is untrue, but I wish it were true.*

• *Get in the way* - a phrase meaning that something prevents you from doing something you want.

• *An armchair sportsman* - somebody who likes and is knowledgeable about sport but doesn't participate.

• *Akin* - an adjective that is a useful alternative to *similar*.

• *Competitive physical activities* - try not to repeat the same words during your response, especially if it is a word used in the question. It is quite difficult not to repeat the word *sport* during this answer, but *competitive physical activities* is a possible alternative.

• *Yes, but with some reservations* - is a great way to start a part one answer. You are giving a direct response and signalling that you are about to qualify it.

• *If a wider variety ... kids would be more likely* - It's not always easy to slip in a conditional during a part one answer but if the opportunity arises then it is a good idea to do so.

Television

Examiner
How often do you watch television?

Candidate
I do now and then. I certainly don't watch TV in the same way that I did when I was younger, or my parents still do. For them, it is the default activity every evening and they can easily watch five hours a night. Nowadays there seem to be many more options for my free time and so TV tends to be a last resort when I have exhausted all other possibilities for entertainment or relaxation.

Examiner
What types of programmes do you watch?

Candidate

I like programmes that inform or make me think. One of the great things about subscription streaming services is that you can be quite choosy. There are some well-produced documentaries available covering a huge range of subjects from world history to rarely-seen wildlife. Rarely do I fail to find something which interests me.

Examiner

What TV programmes are popular in your country?

Candidate

To be honest, I don't really know. I'm tempted to say that everyone loves a non-stop diet of soaps and reality shows, but this may be a lazy caricature of what people enjoy. There is so much variety and so much niche programming these days that it's probably unwise to make sweeping generalisations.

Notes:

• *Now and then* - an alternative for *occasionally* or *sometimes*.

• *Default activity* - this is something that you do because there isn't a better alternative available.

• *Last resort* - an idiom meaning the only choice remaining when no alternatives remain or are available.

• *Choosy* - an informal adjective meaning difficult to please or liking only particular things.

• *Rarely do I find ...* - a negative adverbial followed by the verb inversion.

• *To be honest I don't really know* - It may be that you don't know the answer to a question in your IELTS exam. It's not a problem if you admit this but do make sure that you qualify your lack of knowledge in some way. Either explain why you don't know and/or speculate about what the answer might be. IELTS is not a test of knowledge but a test of your use of English.

• *Diet* - a word that most usually means the type of food that a person eats. It can, however, mean a pastime or activity that somebody usually engages in.

• *Caricature* - this usually means a drawing of somebody in which facial features are exaggerated usually for comic effect. It may also mean a written or spoken description that shows a person or group of people in an oversimplified or distorted way.

• *Niche* - in the answer above it means a speciality programme appreciated only by a few people. You could also have a niche sport or a niche hobby.

• *Sweeping generalisation* - a collocation meaning a statement that is inaccurate because the speaker assumes something which does not apply in all instances.

Reading

Examiner
How often do you read books?

Candidate
I read a little in bed each night before going to sleep. Invariably it's no more than a chapter or two before I doze off, but it does enable me to get through a book every couple of weeks or so. It's considerably more when I am on holiday.

Examiner
What types of books do you prefer to read?

Candidate
Well, I have eclectic tastes in books. I tend to alternate between literary fiction and biography but I'm quite curious about lots of things so there's also a fair sprinkling of non-fiction, anything from world history to travel writing.

Examiner
What did you enjoy reading as a child?

Candidate
I was a voracious and indiscriminate reader as a child. It was anything I could get my hands on really. My preference though was adventure novels. I loved stories about kids finding lost treasure or solving mysteries. They didn't have much literary merit, but it was wonderful escapism for a bored youngster such as me.

Notes:

• *Doze off* - a phrasal verb meaning to start to sleep.

• *Get through* - a phrasal verb that has several meanings. Here it means to finish doing something.

• *Eclectic tastes* - this collocation means a liking for a wide variety of types of a thing. It could refer to books, films, music, etc.

• *Fair sprinkling* - a collocation meaning a small quantity of something.

• *Voracious* - an adjective usually meaning some person or animal who needs to eat a large quantity of food. However, it may also mean, as it does here, a person who engages in something with great enthusiasm.

• *Indiscriminate* - an adjective that means without the use of much thought or planning.

• *Get your hands on* (something) - an idiom meaning to acquire something you want.

If you get the time before the test, here are ten more part one topics with typical questions to consider. Try to think how you would answer them using the inform and qualify method.

Shopping

Do you enjoy shopping?

What is your favourite shop?

Do you ever shop online?

Transport

Do you use public transport?

What is public transport like in your city?

Would you prefer to drive or take a train for a long journey?

Museums and galleries

Do you enjoy visiting museums and galleries?

Do you think that museums and galleries should be free?

Did you enjoy visiting museums as a child?

Music

Do you often listen to music?

What are your favourite types of music?

Do you play a musical instrument?

Holidays

What is your favourite holiday destination?

What holidays did you enjoy as a child?

Do you prefer travelling alone or in a group?

Pets

Do you own a pet?

Did you have pets when you were a child?

What pets are popular in your country?

Weather

What is your favourite season of the year?

What is the weather usually like in your country?

Would you like to move to a place where the weather is different?

Family

Do you spend much time with your family?

What things do you like to do when you are with your family?

Is family important in your country?

Daily routine

What time do you get up in the morning?

What is your favourite part of the day?

Do you have a set daily routine?

Parks and Gardens

Do you visit parks and gardens in your city?

What do you enjoy doing there?

Did you visit parks when you were young?

PART TWO AND THE NARRATIVE+SIX SYSTEM

Part two is sometimes referred to as the *Individual Long Turn* and is perhaps the most feared part of the IELTS speaking exam. But it needn't be. Essentially, the whole purpose of part two is to show the examiner that you are able to speak on a given topic in English naturally and fluently using the types of idiomatic language and grammatical constructions that a native speaker would use. Why students fear this part so much is perhaps its unpredictability. There appear to be hundreds of possible topics and you have no choice but to answer the one given to you. I have heard so many candidates say after the exam that they would have performed better had they been given a different topic but, in reality, if you are well prepared you should do equally well whatever the topic is.

Although there might appear to be an almost infinite variety of different topics, most fall into one of four categories:

- People

- Places

- Things

- Experiences and Events

We will look in detail at each of these and give you the strategies, vocabulary, and grammar needed to tackle all four with confidence. But first, let's look at a sample topic card.

> Describe something you own which is very important to you.
> You should say:
> where you got it from
> how long you have had it for
> what you use it for
> and explain why it is so important to you

This is from ielts.org, the official IELTS website, and is a typical example of a *things* topic. The examiner will hand you the card and will say something very similar to the following:

I'm going to give you a topic and I'd like you to talk about it for one to two minutes. But before you talk you have one minute to think about what you're going to say. You can make notes if you wish. Do you understand?

So part two is for a maximum of three minutes and you will not be speaking for the first one of those. It's not long so you must make the most of each second, and that definitely includes that first minute of thinking and note-taking time.

You will note that the subject of the topic is given in the first line on the card and then there are four supplementary points. For a high band score, you should address each of those four points. You don't have to speak on them in the order given on the card and often your response will be more coherent if you don't.

As for timing, you should aim to be closer to two minutes than one when you are speaking. The more of that precious time you use, the greater will be the opportunity to exhibit your speaking skills. Don't worry about going over the two-minute maximum. The examiner will simply stop you and you won't be penalised. However, you will have robbed yourself of the chance to finish speaking with a definite conclusion. There are advantages to this which we will look at later.

Therefore in your practice sessions use some sort of timing device and try to get as close to the two-minute mark as you can. Very quickly you will become familiar with what two minutes feel like when you are speaking at a natural pace and you will also understand how much, and how little, you can say for each of the four subdivisions of the topic. I have seen some teachers and websites recommend that you glance at your wristwatch during the exam, but you are, in fact, no longer allowed to have a watch with you during any of the four modules.

Don't aim to speak for thirty seconds on each of the four prompts because for some of them, there won't be very much to say. The last one is invariably the most important and it's here where you will have the most scope to incorporate your complex structures and wide vocabulary resource.

The Narrative+Six system

The *Narrative+Six* is a strategic approach to part two. If you follow it, you will score highly for coherence, grammar, and lexical resource. Here's what you need to do:

First, you need to construct a narrative. All this means is that you need to think of a story that will incorporate the four prompts. For many of the cue cards, this will be quite easy. Consider the following first line from a card:

Describe a positive experience you had during your teenage years.

Here you are being invited to tell a story and you will automatically construct a narrative without giving it too much thought. Now consider this prompt:

Describe a useful domestic appliance that you own

It's not easy to tell an interesting story about a refrigerator, but it's not impossible. The cue cards will usually prompt you to talk about the subject in a way that relates to you, in this instance, it needs to be an appliance that you own, but they don't always. Whether they do or not, the easiest way to construct a narrative is to connect the subject matter to yourself in some way. If necessary be inventive. The examiner is neither going to know nor care whether your story is accurate in every detail.

The more interesting the story the better. You won't get extra marks for entertaining the examiner, but it will do absolutely no harm to make your story engaging.

When you have thought of a story you should try to add the following six elements to it:

- Paraphrase

- Phrasal verb

- Narrative tense

- Inversion with Negative Adverbial

- Conditional

- Idiom

I'm not suggesting that this is easy but, with sufficient practice, it will become so, and the following chapters will give you plenty of examples of exactly how these elements can be incorporated into any part two response.

Start your narrative with a paraphrase

Most students tend to start their part two response with, *I'd like to talk about ...* or *I'd like to tell you about...*

Neither are particularly bad ways to begin but nor will they gain you any credit. An alternative is to paraphrase the first line of the prompt. Effective paraphrasing is a specific requirement for grade 7.0 and above and the examiner will be listening for it.

So for, *Describe a positive experience you had during your teenage years*, you could start by saying the following:

Thinking back to a blissfully happy period of my life, what really stands out for me as a teenager was my first high school prom.

Here you are telling the examiner that you are going to talk about a positive experience but without using those two words It also happens to contain two phrasal verbs and in *blissfully happy* a less common adverb and strong collocation.

For, *Describe a useful domestic appliance that you own*, you could start with this:

If I had to pick out one household device which I find the most beneficial I would definitely choose the pride and joy of my kitchen, a toasted sandwich maker.

In one opening sentence, we have paraphrased *useful domestic appliance* by substituting *beneficial household device.* We have used a phrasal verb, a second conditional, and an idiom. The sentence is also an example of hyperbole. A toasted sandwich maker is not something you would usually be proud or joyful about, but I have used deliberate exaggeration to engage the examiner's attention.

Both of these opening sentences can be adapted for many part two cue cards and both contain the types of grammatical devices, vocabulary, and idiomatic language which will impress your examiner. Both are also a more interesting way of starting your talk than saying, *I would like to tell you about my toasted sandwich maker/school dance.* IELTS examiners are highly skilled professionals but they are also human. Try not to bore them.

Please note that occasionally the first line of the card does not lend itself well to paraphrasing. An example is, **Describe a book you have recently read.**
Here I would start by talking about when and where I read my chosen book:

It was last year on holiday when I was relaxing on the beach that I finally got around to reading David Copperfield by Charles Dickens.

If you don't start with a paraphrase then look at the other cue card prompts for an opportunity. In the part two sample responses in the following chapters, there are several examples of this.

End your narrative with a conditional

There are basically three ways to end your part two talk. In order of preference, they are as follows:

• It drifts to an inconclusive finish after one minute because you can't think of anything more to talk about.

• The examiner stops you at the two-minute mark because you are still speaking.

• You finish just before two minutes with a strong, interesting, and grammatically complex statement.

Don't be alarmed if the second of these happens to you. If you have combined the six elements of the system with a wide vocabulary resource, you have nothing to worry about. If, however, you have spoken about all four cue card prompts, and your narrative is reaching a conclusion then a good way to finish is with a conditional. It will bring your talk to a natural conclusion in an interesting way and, if you haven't done so already, will give you the ideal opportunity to incorporate this grammatical device. Here are some examples:

Let's say that you have to describe a restaurant that you like. A good way to finish would be to say to the examiner,

"..... and so if you have the chance while you're in the city I would definitely recommend visiting La Taverna."

If you need to describe a country you would like to visit you can finish with,

".... and so If I was lucky enough to have the opportunity to travel the world, I would definitely visit Brazil."

If you have to describe an important historical event you could conclude with,

"... and so if it had not been for the assassination of Archduke Franz Ferdinand in 1914 the history of the 20th century would have been very different."

Work your way through as many part two questions as you can and try to think of possible endings using a conditional. If you have the time to do this, you will probably increase your speaking band score!

One-minute preparation

The first thing you should get into the habit of doing every time you see a new cue card is to ask yourself what the tense is. It's surprisingly easy to get it wrong when you are anxious. This might seem like obvious advice, but I am frequently surprised during practice sessions with my students how often they fail to spot this crucial piece of information. In particular, a common problem is mistaking the verb tense in the first sentence on the card. Consider the following three:

- Describe something you own

- Describe something you owned

- Describe something you would like to own

Part two topics can talk about present, past, or hypothetical future situations. It's absolutely crucial that you speak about your topic in the correct tense. So, in that one minute of thinking time spend the first couple of seconds establishing what that tense is.

Next, you should plan an outline of your story and then you should think of how you will incorporate the structures of the *Narrative+Six* system. If necessary, make brief notes or bullet points. You simply won't have time to write complete sentences or indeed a complete plan of what you are going to say. The bullet points are merely to keep you on track and remind you to use the structures.

Let's look at this in detail using the card from the official IELTS website. Here it is again:

> Describe something you own which is very important to you.
> You should say:
> where you got it from
> how long you have had it for
> what you use it for
> and explain why it is so important to you

First, we need to establish what the key tense is. This is easy, it's in the present because it's about something you own now. However, it's important to note that we are going to have to use past tenses because we need to explain where we got the thing from and how long we have owned it.

Second, think of your story and, if necessary, be creative. The examiner is not interested in whether your story is true, only in how you use the English language. For this cue card, I'm going to choose to tell the examiner about a watch my father gave me on my eighteenth birthday.

And third, we need to think about how to incorporate the six features of the system. It doesn't matter in which order but it's often best to start with a paraphrase. In this card, it's quite easy to do. The first line has two key elements, *something you own*, and very *important to you*. I'm going to paraphrase these by replacing them with *one of my possessions* and *especially meaningful for me*.

Then I'm going to add a phrasal verb. One that immediately comes to my mind is *hand down*. It means to give an object to a younger generation and it's going to fit perfectly in my story.

For my idiom, I'm going to use *make a big thing of*. It means to exaggerate the importance of something and we usually use it in the negative. I'm going to explain how my father gave me the watch in a quiet way when there was nobody else around He *didn't make a big thing of* the event.

Because I'm going to be telling a story, it's natural that I will be describing a sequence of events. To explain that Dad gave me the watch in the morning after he woke me with my morning cup of tea, I will incorporate a sentence like this - *It was a morning in the middle of the week and Dad had brought me a cup of tea in bed. And then he handed me the watch.* The bringing of the tea is first and signified with the past perfect, and the giving of the watch follows with the past simple.

In my story, I need to explain what I use the watch for and there is an extremely useful negative adverbial construction that is perfect for describing something which does two things. It's *not only ...but also ...* and I'm going to explain that not only does the watch keep perfect time, but it also looks good.

Somewhere in the story, preferably at the end if I feel that I'm close to the two-minute mark, I want to tell the examiner that I would like to give the watch to my own son one day. I don't actually have a son yet, so a first conditional will express my hope perfectly, *if I'm lucky, I will be able to pass it on to my son on his eighteenth birthday*.

I would recommend that you make notes so that you can refer to them when you are speaking to ensure that you don't miss anything. Mine would look something like this:

- *a possession which is especially meaningful*
- *handed down*
- *had brought me tea and then handed me the watch*
- *Dad didn't make a big thing*
- *not only does it keep perfect time but*
- *if I'm lucky, I will pass on*

You are, of course, not limited to using just one of each of these features in your talk. If they are appropriate go ahead and use two or more phrasal verbs or idioms etc. You should also try to incorporate any less common vocabulary that you know.

Here is my sample answer:

If I had to choose one of my possessions which is especially meaningful for me, then it would definitely have to be my vintage watch. Although it's quite old it's not particularly valuable, or at least I don't think it is, but it's an heirloom handed down from my grandfather to my father and now me. I can remember really clearly when Dad gave it to me, it's quite a few years ago now but it seems like yesterday. It was my eighteenth birthday and I was only a few weeks away from leaving school.

It was actually an ordinary school morning in the middle of the week and, as usual, Dad had brought me a cup of tea in bed. And then he handed me the watch. He didn't make a big thing of it, that's not really his style and he doesn't go in for displays of emotion. He just put it in my hand saying, 'My father gave me this on my eighteenth, so I suppose you had better have it now.' It meant far more to me than if he had wrapped it up and presented it to me in front of all the family.

I've had the watch now for seven years and I wear it frequently. Not only does it keep perfect time but, because it's quite plain and unpretentious, it also goes with pretty much any type of clothing or occasion from casual to formal.

And so why is it important to me? Well, it's not because it is a priceless antique because it most definitely isn't. It only has sentimental value and that's because my Dad wore it for many years and I also know that my grandad used to wear it - that was obviously long before I was born. And hopefully, one day, if I'm lucky, I will be able to pass it on to my son on his eighteenth birthday.

This response would score highly for lexical resource. I have used the word *vintage* as an alternative to the very common word *old* and have also described the watch as an *heirloom*, meaning an object passed down through generations of the same family.

Priceless and *unpretentious* are words that have a much more precise meaning than more common alternative words a band six candidate might use such as *expensive* and *simple*.

To recap, here are the six structures from the system.

• I have paraphrased, *Describe something you own which is very important to you* with, *one of my possessions which is especially meaningful for me.*

• There are two phrasal verbs, *hand down* and *pass on*, both meaning to give something to a younger generation

• There is the idiomatic phrase, *to make a big thing of*. This means to exaggerate the importance of something and is usually used in the negative. For example, *I don't like making a big thing of my birthdays.*

• The narrative tense sequence of past perfect plus past simple is in the passage, *Dad had brought me a cup of tea in bed to wake me up. And then he handed me the watch.*

• There is the negative adverbial structure of *not only ... but also. Not only does it keep perfect time but because it's quite plain and unpretentious it also goes with ...*

• There are actually two conditionals, one at the very beginning and one at the end. *If I had to choose one of my possessions which is especially meaningful for me, then it would definitely have to be my vintage watch* and, *if I'm lucky, I will be able to pass it on to my son on his eighteenth birthday.*

I fully appreciate that applying the *Narrative+Six* system doesn't look easy and I readily admit that it isn't to begin with. You might think it's impossible to think how to incorporate the six structures into a story you have to create from a prompt you have never seen before. And all of that in one minute. But I do know from experience that with sufficient practice it gets a lot easier.

Many of the phrases such as *not only ... but also ...* can be reused time after time as can lots of phrasal verbs and idioms. You don't have to know that many.

In the following chapters are a large number of typical part two cue cards and each has my one-minute notes and a sample response. Before reading the response grab a pen and paper, think of a story to go with the prompts, and note down how you would incorporate the six structures of the system. At first, it may take you a lot longer than a minute but don't worry. You will quickly improve.

Your stories will be different from mine, as will be your notes. This obviously doesn't matter. Every card has an unlimited number of possible responses. They are limited only by our imaginations and, if they contain the right elements, all are capable of achieving a high band score.

And finally, in this section, a couple of crucially important points about IELTS speaking are these:

• Do not memorise part two answers. Cue card themes remain the same from year to year, but the prompts do change. The examiners can easily spot when you are reciting from memory and you will score badly. My sample answers are here to help you to understand how to construct a story and incorporate a range of high-scoring grammatical devices. Please don't learn them off by heart!

• Do not attempt complex structures unless you are sure you know how to use them correctly. If in doubt leave them out. Your story should be fluent and coherent, but it won't be if you are struggling to remember how to form a tense or recall when its use is appropriate. If you are in any doubt try if you possibly can to practice with a teacher or native speaker who will be able to tell you if you are using the structures correctly and in a way that sounds natural. The same goes for less-common vocabulary. Simplicity with accuracy is better than complexity with errors.

• Please remember that you are not delivering a lecture. Talking about a random subject for two minutes to a person you have never met before is not something that happens in real life. It's an artificial and, for some, an unsettling situation. But the IELTS exam is supposed to be a conversation, so try to imagine that you are telling an interesting story to a friend.

Rounding off questions

At the end of your talk, the examiner may take the opportunity to finish part two by asking you a couple of what the official IELTS website refers to as *rounding-off questions*. These are very simple questions and there will be a direct connection to what you had chosen to talk about. In the example above of the heirloom watch the examiner might ask the following:

> • *Do you have any other watches that you like to wear?*

> • *I've noticed that people don't tend to wear watches as often as they used to. Why do you think that is?*

Do not be tempted to give long answers to these rounding off questions. This is a part of the IELTS speaking test where one sentence is enough. Save your complex grammar and impressive vocabulary for the other parts and just give a simple response such as these:

- *I've only got one other watch but it's not particularly interesting or valuable, so I sometimes wear it when I'm playing sports.*

- *I've noticed that too and I think it's because everyone has smartphones these days. You don't really need a watch anymore.*

Please note that the examiners don't always ask these rounding-off questions. Don't be concerned, it may be because part two is close to exceeding three minutes and he or she wants to move quickly to part three.

Next, we will examine in detail each of the four principal categories of part two topics looking at strategies to deal with each and the type of vocabulary, idiomatic language, and grammatical structures to get you a high band score. But just before we do here's a way to remember the six structures of the Narrative+Six system:

The **Narrative+Six** mnemonic

A mnemonic (the first m is silent) is a system to help you remember something.

Practising IELTS Conversation Produces Noticeable Improvement

Paraphrase
Idiom
Conditional
Phrasal verb
Narrative tense
Inversion with Negative Adverbial

PEOPLE

Some IELTS part two topics seem to be considerably more popular with students than others and, from my experience, people topics are the most popular of all. Describing people is considered to be relatively easy, and I assume it is because we all have friends and family members that we can easily call to mind and talk about. It is much the same with people that we know less well on a personal basis but perhaps encounter professionally, such as teachers. Even people that we have never met, like famous musicians or politicians, are also easily described.

Having said all that, being able quickly to think of somebody to talk about when handed a cue card is not the same as being able to talk about them in a way that will earn you a high band score. You will still need to employ the same strategies and display the same complexities of language that you would use if you were describing a less familiar and more 'difficult' topic. If anything you need to be particularly careful when talking about what you feel is an undemanding subject that you don't slip into undemanding language. Hopefully, this chapter will enable you to avoid falling into that trap.

First a few general words about people topics. As with all part two topics, the emphasis will be on the positive. You are rarely going to be asked directly about people that you dislike or disapprove of.

People - by personal characteristics

We can divide the people we are asked to describe into two categories - by their personal characteristics and by their skills, job, or interests. In the first category, the majority of the cue card prompts will ask us to describe people personally know to us and these will invariably be members of our family or our friends. The questions are often about our personal relationships with these people and relate to why we like or admire them.

This category can be further divided by age. Mostly we are asked about a friend/family member who is of a specific generation, but we may also be given a wider choice. The following cue card does that and, when I use it in practice tests with my students, it's a popular one. Most candidates shouldn't have too much difficulty selecting somebody to talk about.

Describe a member of your family who you admire.
You should say:
who the person is
what they do
what their best quality is
and explain why you admire that person so much

Strategy

The overwhelming majority of people cue cards are set firmly in the present day. There are occasional exceptions, for example when we are asked to talk about a famous historical figure, but if we are required to describe family members or other people personally known to us then it is inevitable that we will be dealing with the here and now. As with all part two topics, the emphasis will be on the positive and the optimistic; the examiners will not take the risk of negativity by asking you about family members no longer living.

This, however, does not and should not, prevent us from using a range of past tenses to describe what the living person has done in the past. So during your one minute select a family member who will give you plenty of scope for using a range of tenses, and also for displaying plenty of interesting vocabulary and idiomatic language. Personally, I would select an older person because they have usually done more in their lives, but it doesn't have to be.

Describing a family member that you like and admire should be relatively easy but be careful that you don't simply use a string of synonyms for *nice*. So telling the examiner that, for example, your grandfather is very kind, generous, and helpful and that he's always friendly and affectionate is not going to win you lots of points for lexical resource. By all means, as part of your preparation for the speaking test, make lists of useful adjectives but use them judiciously. Remember that the examiner is looking for skilful and precise use of your lexical resource.

The best strategy for describing people is to tell a story as I have done in the sample answer. Virtually all part two answers can be turned into simple narratives which tends to make them interesting to listen to and obliges you to use narrative tenses. The following sample answer is a story of a young man from a poor background who works hard, gets married, and eventually has grandchildren. This describes why I admire him rather than simply giving a list of his virtues.

One-minute notes

- the relative I respect
- paternal grandfather
- wrong side of the tracks
- having worked hard ... he earned
- worked his way up
- rarely is he meddlesome

Sample answer

Without a doubt, the relative I respect the most is my paternal grandfather. He didn't have a particularly auspicious background, in fact, if I'm honest with you he grew up on the wrong side of the tracks. But he was always determined to better himself - I suppose it's because he had first-hand experience of the disadvantages of being poor.

And so having worked hard at school he earned a place at college. He must have been the first in his family to do so. And then he got quite a run-of-the-mill job with a small accountancy firm, he was just a pen-pusher really. But he worked hard and put in the hours and gradually worked his way up in the company. He met my gran there, she was a typist I think, and the rest is history. I'm not going to say that they lived happily ever after but it's near enough.

I've always loved spending time with them both, Granddad especially. He's a gentleman of leisure now and has loads of hobbies and interests but he still seems to have lots of time for everyone else. That's what I admire about him the most I suppose. When I was a kid, whenever I needed help with anything like homework, especially anything to do with maths, he was always there for me. He invariably made time even though he had four other demanding grandchildren.

And he still does make the time. I don't get to see him now as often as I like but even now he really takes an interest in what I'm doing and is ready to give advice, but only if I ask for it – rarely is he meddlesome. One day it would be nice to have grandchildren of my own. If I did, I hope that I would treat them just like he's always treated me.

Points to note

- *the relative I respect*
A paraphrase of the words in the question – *a member of your family who you admire*

- *paternal grandfather*
If talking about your grandparents it's good to identify which ones. Your paternal

grandparents are your father's parents. The parents of your mother are your maternal grandparents.

• *wrong side of the tracks*
This is an idiom meaning an impoverished and undesirable part of a town.

• *auspicious*
An adjective meaning favourable.

• *run-of-the-mill*
An idiom meaning ordinary.

• *pen-pusher*
This is a person who performs routine and perhaps tedious work in an office. It has negative connotations.

• *put in the hours*
A phrase meaning to work very long hours.

• *having worked hard ... he earned*
A sequence of events indicated by a perfect participle followed by a past simple.

• *worked his way up*
Work up is a phrasal verb with a number of meanings. Here it means to progress towards something better through hard work.

• *the rest is history*
If you use the phrase, *the rest is history*, when telling a story it indicates that you do not intend to give further details because either it is too complicated or because they are already well-known.

• *they lived happily ever after*
A phrase most often used at the end of children's stories to indicate that people spent the rest of their lives in happiness.

• *rarely is he meddlesome*
A negative adverbial followed by verb inversion.

• *If I did, I hope that I would*
If you can it's always good to end with a conditional.

Cue cards with similar themes

Preparing in advance to talk about a person older than you in a positive way will definitely be time well spent. The vocabulary, idioms, and grammar of the sample answer above could be adapted easily to fit the following cue cards all of which are from past IELTS speaking tests:

Describe somebody in your family who you like.
You should say:
how this person is related to you
what this person looks like
what kind of person he or she is
and explain why you like this person

Describe an old person that you know.
You should say:
what your relationship is to this person
how often you see them
what people think about this person
and explain why you like them

Describe an older member of your family who you like to spend time with.
You should say:
when you are together
how often you are together
what you do together
and explain why you like to spend time with them

Describe someone you know who you think is a good parent.
You should say:
who they are
how you know them
what children they have
and explain why you think they are a good parent

Having looked in detail at a generic older person answer, let's examine a sample for one of our peers or contemporaries. Preparing a response to a question about somebody personally known to you and who is of your own age is highly recommended.

> Describe a friend who you like to spend time with.
> You should say:
> when and how you met
> how often you see this friend
> what kind of personality your friend has
> and explain why you like to spend time with this friend

Strategy

Again, like most people questions, this one is set in the present, but you are also asked about the past. Just like the grandfather response above, the best way of dealing with this is by telling a story. Hopefully, you won't have any difficulty thinking about who to talk about which will mean you will be able to use all your one-minute thinking of interesting vocabulary and grammatical constructions.

One-minute notes

- enjoy hanging out with
- bawling her head off
- She was finding ... probably because she had been
- rarely do we get the chance ...
- If we had stayed in the same place ... we would meet every day

Sample answer

The friend who I most enjoy hanging out with is Lucy. We met on our first day of primary school. This was a long time ago, ancient history really, but in some respects it seems like yesterday. I can still see Lucy being brought into the classroom by the teacher and the poor girl was bawling her head off. Big tears were dripping down her cheeks and she was dragging her heels. She was obviously finding the whole thing pretty traumatic, probably because she had been separated from her mum. We laugh about it now, especially because she's in the police and doesn't take any nonsense from anyone.

We were inseparable as kids and did everything together. My mother always said we were joined at the hip. I think it was mainly because we've always had the same sort of interests and a similar crazy sense of humour. I've got a strong sense of the ridiculous which she shares. I've lost track of the countless occasions we've been in hysterical laughter together over the years. Lucy can be very serious and responsible at times - she has to be in her job - but she can also be a barrel of laughs.

Recently I left my home town to go to university and she joined the police force in a different city, so rarely do we get the chance to see each other. If we had stayed in the same place, I'm sure we would meet every day. But we still make every effort to spend breaks and holidays with each other. We're going to Ibiza in August and I know we'll have a ball. True friendship like ours is a precious thing and you have to make the most of it.

Points to note

• *enjoy hanging out with*
This paraphrases, *like spending time with,* in the cue card. I didn't replace *friend* because none of the synonyms such as *companion, mate,* or *buddy* have the right connotations for this story. Don't replace words with synonyms unless you are sure they sound right. *Hang out* is a relatively modern and informal phrasal verb. Don't use it in your writing exam.

• *ancient history*
A collocation used informally to indicate that something was a long time ago and the details are no longer important.

• *bawling her head off*
An idiom meaning crying and screaming. It's usually used in connection with young children.

• *dragging her heels*
An idiom indicating that somebody is going somewhere unwillingly.

• *She was finding ... probably because she had been*
Past continuous plus past perfect to indicate a sequence of events.

• *joined at the hip*
An idiom meaning that two people are inseparable friends.

• *a sense of the ridiculous*
A collocation used to mean that somebody has a crazy sense of humour.

• *lose track of*
A phrase meaning that you no longer remember all the details of something.

• *barrel of laughs*
An informal phrase meaning a source of amusement and pleasure.

• *rarely do we get the chance ...*
Negative adverbial followed by inversion.

• *If we had stayed in the same place ... we would meet every day*
A mixed conditional - present result of a past condition.

• *Have a ball*
An informal phrase meaning to enjoy yourself greatly.

Cue cards with similar themes

By making only minimal changes you should be able to adapt Lucy's story to fit the following questions:

> Describe a person who you like to spend time with.
> You should say:
> how you first met
> how often you are together
> what personal characteristics he or she has that you like
> and explain why you like to spend time with this person

> Describe a friend you haven't seen for a long time but who you would like to see again.
> You should say:
> who this friend is
> when you last saw him or her
> what you would like to do together
> and explain why you haven't been in contact for a long time

Let's now prepare a response to a cue card asking about a child or person younger than yourself. These are less common, and you are also less likely to know a child than people of your own age. Hopefully, you have a niece or nephew or friend's child that you can talk about but, if not, it shouldn't be too difficult to be creative. Here's a fairly typical generic child cue card.

> Describe a child that you know.
> You should say:
> who the child is
> how you know the child
> when you see the child
> and explain why you like or dislike this child

Strategy

Although typical in most respects, this card is somewhat unusual in that it offers you the opportunity to speak about somebody in a negative way. I personally wouldn't take that opportunity because I prefer to speak about a person's positive qualities.

One-minute notes

- the youngster I'm most familiar with
- over the moon
- I was studying at university when he was born
- If I had the chance, I would love …
- rarely can you fob him off

Sample answer

I suppose that the youngster I'm most familiar with is my nephew Oliver. He's my big sister and brother-in-law's oldest child and he's just turned five - he started at his primary school last September. He was my parents' first grandchild and therefore my first nephew so all of us in the family were incredibly excited when Ollie was born. Mum and Dad were absolutely over the moon and they spoil him rotten.

I was studying at university when he was born so I didn't get to see him as often as I would have liked when he was a baby but, because my sister and her husband live in the same town as us, I did manage to visit during the vacations. It was amazing to see how much he'd grown and developed from one holiday to the next. One minute he was just a little helpless baby and the next he was a toddler getting into everything and generally causing chaos.

I still see Ollie when I go home for Christmas and family celebrations and it's always one of the highlights of my visits. If I had the chance, I would love to see more of him because I'm fascinated by how inquisitive and endlessly curious he is about everything. He drives my sister mad because he's always taking things to bits to see how they work. And the questions, gosh, he never stops. Rarely can you fob him off with trite answers. He'll keep on at you until he's satisfied and sometimes it's really difficult. Last Christmas he asked me where electricity comes from.

And I love the way that for him, everything is new and exciting. He's as bright as a button and he gets so enthusiastic about things we take for granted. Being with him is like seeing the world through a different pair of eyes. I know my sister is apprehensive, but I suspect he's going to be great fun to be with when he's a teenager.

Points to note

• *the youngster I'm most familiar with*
A paraphrase of *a child that you know.*

• *over the moon*
An idiom meaning overjoyed.

• *spoil rotten*
An idiom meaning to give somebody everything they ask for. Often used to describe how grandparents indulge their grandchildren.

• *I was studying at university when he was born*
Narrative sequence of past continuous followed by past simple.

• *toddler*
A child aged between approximately one and three years.

• *If I had the chance, I would love ...*
A second conditional.

• *drive somebody mad*
A phrase meaning to annoy or irritate somebody.

• *rarely can you ...*
Negative adverbial followed by verb inversion.

• *keep on at* (somebody)
A phrasal verb meaning to annoy a person by making repeated requests.

• *fob off*
An informal phrasal verb meaning to give somebody an untrue or incomplete answer to a question in the hope that they will stop asking.

• *bright as a button*
This idiom is used to describe a very clever, happy, and lively person, usually a child.

• *to see the world through a different pair of eyes*
A phrase meaning to see the world around you in a different way.

• I don't, incidentally, have a nephew but it was relatively easy to construct a story about a lively toddler - I've seen enough of them in films.

People – by skills, job, or interests

In addition to being asked to describe people known to you in terms of their character or personality, as in the examples above, you may also be invited to talk about a person's job, interests, or a particular skill or accomplishment. Usually, these are people known to us, but a common variant is to be asked about a famous person that we know about but not in a personal capacity. The majority of these topics are set in the present and concern living people but very occasionally we may be asked about a famous person from history.

Let's start with a person known to us who has a particular hobby or interest.

> Describe someone you know who enjoys outdoor activities.
> You should say:
> who the person is
> what activities he or she does
> how often he or she does these activities
> and explain why you think he or she enjoys outdoor activities

Strategy

If you can't think of someone you know who likes outdoor activities, then there's no reason why you couldn't reuse some of the basic details you had prepared for a more general question on somebody of your own age and improvise. The key to success with people cue cards is being able to embellish a basic character study with details that address the specific points on the card. For this sample, I am going to use the example of a personal friend.

One-minute notes

- a friend who is mad about open-air recreation
- rarely did she play
- given half a chance she would play football
- calm down
- she managed to fit this in while she was studying

Sample answer

I have a friend who is mad about open-air recreation. Her name is Sue and we went to the same junior school from the age of about five. Back then she was a bit of a tomboy and she much preferred climbing trees than doing typically girlie things – rarely did she play with dolls for example. She adored all types of sport and I remember her getting into trouble with her mother because she used to go home most evenings caked in mud. Given half a chance she would play football with the boys after school.

We went on to the same high school and she started to calm down a bit and even began to study hard. But she also found out that she had a talent for running. Not short distance or sprinting but cross country and endurance type events. One of the sports teachers really encouraged her and she developed a real passion for it. She joined an athletics club and used to go training most days. Somehow, she managed to fit this in while she was studying, and she did really well in her exams.

We went to different universities, but we still kept in touch and I know that it was at university that she started training for marathons. I don't think she ever really came close to running for her country or anything that serious, but she goes all over the world taking part in marathons and she's raised loads for charity.

And why does she enjoy it? I did actually ask her this the last time I saw her, and she said that although she delights in the fresh air and the feeling of freedom when she's running, the best thing was the feeling of accomplishment when she crossed the finish line. And I suppose that's as good a reason as any.

Points to note

• *a friend who is mad about open-air recreation*
This paraphrases *someone you know who enjoys outdoor activities.*

• *mad about*
An informal phrasal verb meaning very enthusiastically fond of something or somebody.

• *tomboy*
A girl who likes rough outdoor activities traditionally associated with young boys.

• *rarely did she play*
Negative adverbial followed by verb inversion.

• *Given half a chance she would play football*
This combines an implied condition – the if clause is not stated here – with a very useful idiomatic phrase. If someone would do something *given half a chance*, they would do it if the opportunity came up.

•*caked in mud*
A phrase and collocation meaning covered in dirt or mud.

• *calm down*
A phrasal verb meaning to become more quiet and composed.

• *she managed to fit this in while she was studying*
A narrative sequence – past simple and past continuous.

• *find out*
This phrasal verb means that you learn something you did not already know.

• *keep in touch*
To make an effort to maintain contact with another person even if you are living some distance apart.

• *that's as good a reason as any*
A common phrase indicating that the reason given is as good as, or no worse than, possible alternatives.

• Note the rhetorical question right at the end - *and why does she enjoy it?* This is an excellent way to bring your talk to a definite conclusion and reminds the examiner that you are clearly addressing what is perhaps the most important question on the cue card.

Here are some more sample hobbies, interests, and skills cue cards for you to think about:

> Describe someone you know who collects things.
> You should say:
> what they collect
> how the collection is stored
> how long they have had the collection
> and explain why they enjoy collecting that thing

> Talk about a person you know who can speak two languages.
> You should say:
> who the person is
> how long you have known them
> what languages they can speak
> and explain why it is helpful to speak more than one language

In addition to hobbies and interests, we may also be asked about a person's job or profession. We'll start with one that we are going to have personal experience of, either currently or in the past, that of a teacher.

Describe someone you think is a good teacher.
You should say:
who the teacher is
how you know them
what they teach
and explain why you think they are a good teacher

Strategy

Hopefully, there is a teacher from your past who was good at his or her job but, if not, you should be aware of what are the qualities of a good teacher and improvise. It does happen in IELTS speaking part two that you might not have direct personal experience of something that you are being asked but, with good preparation, you should be able to be creative. Note that we are asked to describe somebody who is a good teacher in the present day. I'm going to talk about somebody from my school days, but I'll make it clear to the examiner that I have read the card and so will refer to the teacher still working now.

One-minute notes

- the best of the many tutors
- he was still teaching there recently, and I met him
- never did he talk down to us
- bored to tears
- If all the teachers had been as engaging ... I would be much better informed

Sample answer

They say that you never forget a good teacher and I think it's true. I can easily recall the best of the many tutors we had during my high school days. He's still teaching there, and I met him at an alumni reunion, but he must be close to retirement now. His name is Mr. White, though we had to call him 'Sir', but I suppose like most teachers he had a nickname. His was 'Chalky' - a bit obvious for a teacher called 'White' I suppose

He was my history tutor all through my high school years, so I knew him right from being a really young kid all the way to being an older teenager - I had just turned eighteen when I left school. He taught all aspects of world history from about the time of the Romans through to the present. But he was actually a bit of a polymath because he seemed to know about everything. He had a habit of digressing from the lesson to talk about a variety of subjects.

He had some great stories and they were always about things that we found fascinating. Sometimes we just sat there spellbound listening to him. What I remember as well is that he was never condescending. Never did he talk down to us but always spoke as if we were equals. I think that's why he never seemed to have the problems with discipline that some of his colleagues did. I shudder to think now how badly behaved we could often be, but I think it was because we were bored to tears half the time. If all the teachers had been as engaging as Mr. White, I would be much better informed about subjects other than history. Chalky never bored us. We just sat there and took everything in.

And that's why I think he was a great teacher and if I ever have children, I hope they'll be lucky enough to have inspirational educators like him.

Points to note

• *the best of the many tutors*
A paraphrase for a *good teacher*.

• *he was still teaching there recently, and I met him*
A narrative sequence of past continuous and past simple.

• *I had just turned eighteen when I left school*
There's no reason why you shouldn't include more than one narrative sequence if you are able. This is past perfect followed by past simple.

• *polymath*
A person who has knowledge of a wide variety of subjects.

• *spellbound*
Enthralled and fascinated by something.

• *never did he talk down to us*
A combination of a phrasal verb and a negative adverbial. If you *talk down* to someone it means you speak to them in a simple way as if they are unlikely to understand.

• *shudder to think*
A phrase used for saying that you are unwilling to think about something because it is unpleasant.

• *bored to tears*
An idiom meaning extremely bored.

• *If all the teachers had been as engaging ... I would be much better informed*
This is a mixed conditional – the present result of a past condition.

• *take everything in*
The phrasal verb *to take in* has many meanings. Here it means to understand and remember something you hear or read.

• *if I ever have children, I hope they'll be lucky enough to …*
A simple first conditional to finish.

• As in the example of the grandfather who was generous with his time, it is better to describe the reasons why you consider a person to have good qualities in terms of a narrative instead of simply listing those qualities. Simply saying that your teacher was *calm, patient, kind, and inspirational* will not fill enough time nor will it gain you many points for vocabulary.

• Idioms for describing boredom are often useful. *Bored to tears* is a common idiomatic phrase but we could also say that something, like a lesson, for example, is *as dull as ditchwater*.

• When describing things or people that are interesting, which we often have to do in IELTS, try to avoid using the word *interesting* itself too often. It is far too common and there are lots of excellent alternatives such as *spellbinding, captivating, enthralling, beguiling, and engrossing*.

Similar questions

The example of the history teacher Mr. White could be adapted and modified for these topic cue cards. Try to collect phrases and vocabulary suitable for people's occupations, especially vocabulary with positive connotations.

> **Describe someone you know who has an interesting job.**
> **You should say:**
> **who the person is**
> **how you know this person**
> **what job they do**
> **and explain why you think this person's job is interesting**
>
> **Talk about a person you know whose job is important to society.**
> **You should say:**
> **who the person is**
> **what their job is**
> **what they do at work**
> **and explain why their job is important to society**

Mr. White could even be the basis for these topics:

> Describe someone who has had an important influence on your life.
> You should say:
> who the person is
> how long you have known him or her
> what qualities this person has
> and explain why they have had such an influence on you

> Describe a very intelligent person you know.
> You should say:
> who the person is
> when and where you first met him or her
> what kind of person he or she is
> and explain why you think this person is intelligent

The majority of cue cards in the people category will, like all the examples above, ask you about those that you personally know. Occasionally, however, you will be asked about those that you don't. These will either be living people who are famous for something or a figure from history. Let's start with a typical example of the former:

> Describe an artist or an entertainer that you admire.
> You should say:
> who they are and what they do
> how they became successful
> How you found out about them
> and explain why you admire them

Strategy

This cue card gives you a lot of scope. The word *artist* can have a number of meanings, the most common being a person who produces works of art such as a painter or sculptor. It can also mean a writer or poet. An entertainer could be a singer, dancer, or television presenter.

The card doesn't specify that the person has to be famous, and many living artists aren't. Nor does it specifically say that you shouldn't talk about a friend or somebody you know personally. It is, after all, not impossible that you personally know an artist or performer of some kind. However, the fifth line on the card gives you a big clue that this is not what the question intends. *Find out* is a phrasal verb meaning to obtain some information about something or somebody.

You would not necessarily be penalised heavily for describing your friend who happens to be a singer or performer, but it's clear that this is not what the examiner is expecting you to talk about. As always, read every line in the card carefully.

One-minute notes

- a performer I hold in high regard
- tried his hand
- if the common room television hadn't been on
- not only does he present variety shows
- we became engrossed in a quiz show that he was hosting.
- comes across

Sample answer

I don't watch a lot of television but a performer I hold in high regard is a man called Bradley Walsh. He's definitely an all-rounder and it's difficult to put him into a particular category of entertainer. I think he actually started his career as a footballer but when he got too old for that he hosted game shows on daytime television. Not many people watch these, but he was very popular and decided to move into acting. He got a part in one of our most popular evening soaps which inevitably meant that he quickly became a household name. Since then he seems to have tried his hand at lots of things. Not only does he present variety shows on TV but he's also a singer - mainly covers of jazz standards.

I found out about him by chance when I was a student. If the common room television hadn't been on one afternoon, I probably wouldn't know about him. It was a custom for us to take a break for coffee and on this particular occasion, we became engrossed in a quiz show on TV that he was hosting. It was a bit cheesy but great fun and I've since learned that it had a bit of a cult following in universities. We all had great fun shouting out the answers to his questions.

I think he mainly appeals to people of my parents' age - that's definitely his target market - but I can't help but admire him. He's obviously immensely talented and also amazingly quick-witted on live shows. But he also comes across as being genuinely likeable. It might just be an act, but he seems as though he is actually interested in the ordinary people that he has on his shows.

Points to note

- *a performer I hold in high regard*
A paraphrase of *entertainer that I admire.*

- *all-rounder*
A versatile person.

- *soaps*
Television drama serials.

- *household name*
A person who is well-known by the public.

- *we became engrossed in a quiz show that he was hosting.*
A narrative sequence of past simple plus past continuous.

- *tried his hand*
An idiom meaning to do an activity for the first time in order to discover whether you like it or are good at it.

- *if the common room television hadn't been on ... I probably wouldn't know about him.*
A mixed conditional indicating the present result of a past condition.

- *Not only does he present variety shows*
Not only ... but also ... is a very useful negative adverbial structure that can be incorporated into many part two responses

- *cheesy*
An informal adjective meaning that something lacks quality or style and is perhaps somewhat silly. It doesn't have to have a wholly negative connotation. It's perfectly possible to enjoy something that is cheesy.

- *cult following*
If something, like a TV show, film or band has a cult following it means that it has a small group of passionate fans.

- *quick-witted*
able to reply in a clever and amusing way without thinking for a long time.

- *comes across*
A phrasal verb meaning to behave in a way that makes others think that you have a particular characteristic. So, if somebody *comes across* as being pleasant, it means that they act in that way, but it doesn't necessarily mean that they genuinely are pleasant.

Here are some similar cue cards where you could recycle some of your material:

Describe your favourite singer.
You should say:
who the person is
what type of songs he or she sings
what type of people listen to his or her songs
and explain why he or she is your favourite singer

Describe a TV presenter that you like
You should say:
who he or she is
what programme he or she presents
how he or she presents this programme
and explain why you like this TV presenter

Describe someone in the news you would like to meet.
You should say:
who the person is
what they do
why they are in the news
and explain why you would like to meet them

Talk about a famous person you would like to meet
You should say:
who the person is
why he or she is famous
why you would like to meet this person
and explain what you would do if you met him or her

And finally, in this category let's look at the only time you are likely to be asked about a person who is no longer living - when they are a famous person from history.

Describe a historical figure who you know about.
You should say:
who the person is
where and when he or she lived
what this person is remembered for
and explain his or her contribution to the world

Strategy

This is another cue card that gives you a lot of scope, but note from the fourth and fifth lines of the card that you are clearly intended to describe somebody no longer alive, and also somebody who made a positive contribution to history, so no evil dictators! Apart from that, there is no reason why your historical figure shouldn't be an artist, writer, or inventor. A famous leader would certainly be appropriate, but it doesn't have to be. Also note that although the card doesn't specifically ask you to explain why you like or are interested in the person, you may mention why you do. As long as you cover all the points there is no reason not to add extra information if you have time and it is relevant.

One-minute notes

- A celebrated person from the past I'm familiar with
- go through
- closed book
- while he was living there that he started to act
- Not only did he invent a lot of words, but we also use quotes from his plays
- I'm sure that if he was writing now, he would be

Sample answer

A celebrated person from the past I'm familiar with is William Shakespeare. He's said to be one of the greatest playwrights of all time and certainly the preeminent writer in the English language. He's famous for a number of reasons. First, because his works encompass a number of different genres like comedy, tragedy, and history. And secondly, because he wrote about a gamut of emotions and situations that are real to most of us today. All of us at some time in our lives go through such things as unrequited love and grief and possibly even revenge and jealousy. Even though he was writing hundreds of years ago, and we might find the language a bit difficult, we can still all relate to how the characters are feeling and why they act in the ways that they do.

But I think the main reason why he is still so well-known is because most of us studied Shakespeare in school and his plays are still performed. We are all familiar with the stories of his most prominent dramas such as Romeo and Juliet and lots of them have been turned into films. It's such a great plot that there are other spin-offs like ballets and musicals.

His life is something of a closed book, but we do know that he was born in Stratford upon Avon in the sixteenth century. He later moved to London and it was while he was living there that he started to act and write.

As for his contribution to the world, well he's certainly influenced the English language in a big way. Not only did he invent a lot of words, but we also use quotes from his plays on a daily basis even though we probably don't realise where they are from. And he has also influenced many other writers who have adapted his themes and characters. It's astonishing to think that even a Disney film for children like The Lion King is connected to Shakespeare's Hamlet. I'm sure that if he was writing now he would be a Hollywood screenwriter.

Points to note

• *A celebrated person from the past I'm familiar with*
This paraphrases *a historical figure who you know about.*

• *Preeminent*
Very distinguished or surpassing all other people.

• *Gamut of emotions*
This is a collocation and means a wide range of emotions.

• *go through*
A phrasal verb with a number of meanings. Here it means to undergo a difficult experience.

• *unrequited love*
A collocation meaning your love for another person which is not reciprocated.

• *turned into*
A phrasal verb meaning *transformed into.*

• *spin-offs*
A film, TV programme, or other creative work that uses characters or other elements from a previous work.

• *closed book*
An idiom meaning a subject or a person you know very little about. I don't know very much about where and when Shakespeare lived so my answer to this part of the question is quite short. This is perfectly okay. Just make sure you mention each of the points on the cue card and compensate for your shorter responses by expanding on the others.

• *it was while he was living there that he started to act*
A narrative sequence of past continuous followed by past simple.

• *Not only did he invent a lot of words, but we also use quotes from his plays*
A negative adverbial followed by an inversion.

- *I'm sure that if he was writing now he would be*
A second conditional conclusion.

And finally in this section, here is a variation on the theme of people from history:

> Describe a historical figure.
> You should say:
> who he or she is
> why he or she is famous
> why you like or dislike this person
> and briefly describe his or her life

PLACES

The majority of the cue cards in this category will ask you to talk about places that you have visited and are familiar with, and so we will deal with those first. They can be subdivided as follows:

- Countries

- Cites

- Historical or culturally interesting places
monuments, museums, and art galleries

- The natural world
the countryside, coast, rivers, gardens, and parks

- Places you know or visit as part of your regular routine
shops, restaurants, libraries, your own home

Countries

Assuming that you have visited and are familiar with at least one foreign country this should be a relatively easy topic and the following card gives you the opportunity to talk about a wide range of experiences.

> Describe a foreign country you have been to.
> You should say:
> where the country is
> when you went there
> what you did there
> and explain why this is a good country to visit

Strategy

I have always considered that places cue cards test your powers of description to their limits. You could be asked to talk about somewhere as small as your bedroom or as big as a whole country. Quite clearly, if you have only two minutes to describe a whole country, what you did during your visit, and why you would recommend it to others, then the problem is not going to be a lack of things to say but knowing what to omit. The key to success with this cue card is to adopt what we might call a broad-brush strategy. Basically, this means that you won't have the time for too much detail. A general description is sufficient, and the easiest approach is to tell a fairly basic story covering each of the points on the card in turn.

One-minute notes

- visit a number of countries during my travels abroad
- after we had flown into Rome my father hired a car
- looking back
- scratch the surface
- only in later years … did I
- given the chance, I would visit every year.

Sample answer

I've been lucky enough to visit a number of countries during my travels abroad but the one I should like to tell you about is Italy, a country in southern Europe in the heart of the Mediterranean Sea. It's a fascinating and exceptionally beautiful country that I have returned to often, but I first went with my parents when I was about sixteen. After we had flown into Rome my father hired a car so that we could tour around the major cities. Looking back, it probably wasn't such a wise idea because we only had a week's holiday and a couple of days in each place was nothing like enough. We barely scratched the surface of what each had to offer. I mean you could easily spend a month in Rome and still keep finding new things to see.

Anyway, on that first visit, we did a lightning tour of the major monuments such as the Coliseum and St Peter's before heading off to Florence and Milan. It was all a bit of a blur when I think back. All I can really remember is Dad lining us up in front of some cathedral or palace and taking a few photographs before racing to the next place.

Only in later years when I revisited Italy did I come to appreciate what a wonderful country it is. First, if you're interested in art, it's an absolute cultural haven with probably the finest Renaissance paintings and sculptures in the world. Second, you have a wide variety of landscapes from mountains and lakes to miles of breath-taking coastline. And last, but not least, is the food. Italian cuisine is renowned throughout the world and rightly so with each region having interesting and delicious specialities. In short, it's a country that has something for everyone and given the chance, I would revisit every year.

Points to note

- *I've been lucky enough to visit a number of countries during my travels abroad*
A near paraphrase of the first line of the prompt. I have chosen not to replace *country* because possible synonyms, such as *nation*, sound a little unnatural here.

• *After we had flown into Rome my father hired a car*
The narrative tense sequence of past perfect followed by past simple.

• *Look back* and *think back.*
These are extremely useful phrasal verbs and it's likely that you can use either when talking about a personal experience in the past. They are interchangeable and native speakers use both frequently.

• *to scratch the surface*
An idiom meaning to do something in only a very superficial and inadequate way.

• *a lightning tour*
A collocation meaning a very quick tour. It's similar to a *lightning visit.*

• *head off*
Many phrasal verbs have a number of possible meanings, as does this one. In this story, it is an informal alternative to the verb *leave.*

• *a bit of a blur*
This idiomatic phrase means that you are unable to clearly remember the details of an event.

• *Only in later years when I revisited Italy did I ...*
This is a negative adverbial construction.

• *given the chance, I would visit every year.*
Conditionals don't always have to have the *if* word. This is an example of an implied conditional. *Given the chance* implies *if I had the chance*

Cue cards with similar themes

If you are able to talk about a foreign country in general terms, then you should be able to adapt and add to your material in order to approach these cue cards with confidence:

> **Describe a foreign culture that you like**
> **You should say:**
> **what culture it is**
> **how you know about it**
> **how that culture differs from yours**
> **and explain why you like that foreign culture**

Describe an interesting holiday destination
You should say:
what the place is
what can you see and do there
what time of year is it better to be there
and explain why you like it

Describe a place where you enjoyed learning about another culture.
You should say:
what place it was
why you went there
why you learned
and explain why you enjoyed learning about this culture

Although the following cue cards, strictly speaking, belong in the experiences category of part two topics there is absolutely no reason why you shouldn't adapt material that you have prepared for the places category.

Talk about a holiday or vacation you spent with a group of other people.
You should say:
When you had this vacation
Where you went
What you did
and explain how you felt about having a vacation with them

Describe a trip you have taken recently.
You should say:
Where you went
Who you went with
why you went there
and describe some things you saw and did on your trip

Describe the best holiday you ever had.
You should say:
When and where you had it
How you travelled there
What you did on this holiday
and explain why it was so special

Cities

Here's a fairly typical cities cue card:

> Describe your favourite city.
> You should say:
> what is the name of the city and where it is located
> when you visited it
> what are the attractive places of this city
> and explain what influence the city had on you

Strategy

This cue card doesn't specify whether this city should be in your own country or abroad. If you have sufficient time, then prepare an answer for both. However, if you have limited time, choose a city in your country and preferably one which is historically interesting. You will have more opportunities to recycle the material. As always, carefully note the verb tenses on the card. You need to describe the city in the present tense but, in addition, talk about a visit there in the past.

One-minute notes

- city I adore above all others
- never before have I
- it was while I was exploring that I came across
- off the Beaten track
- delve into
- if it hadn't been for that visit then ...

Sample answer

The city I adore above all others is undoubtedly Edinburgh, the capital of Scotland. It's located in the south-east of the country and I first visited it for a long weekend a couple of years ago. I knew quite a lot about it and had seen photographs, but the pictures didn't really do the place justice. It's breathtakingly stunning, especially if you arrive by rail as I did. The station is right in the heart of the city and you emerge into Princes Street, which is the principal thoroughfare. It's a very handsome street with grand hotels and department stores on one side and on the other are gardens set in a valley. Beyond is the ancient castle which sits on top of a hill and dominates the skyline. Never before have I been so impressed by a first view of a city.

During the next couple of days, I didn't really have a set itinerary but just wandered around the older parts of the city. It was while I was exploring that I came across some pretty little alleyways and quaint buildings which in the distant past housed working people. I suspect they are very desirable residences now.

In addition to the major tourist attraction of the medieval castle, the city is also home to a royal palace and a ruined monastery but because of the crowds at those places, I preferred to stay off the beaten track and delve into the quieter quarters. A particular delight for me was a part of the city called the New Town which has some extremely elegant eighteenth-century classical buildings. The proportions of the pillared facades are very pleasing to the eye.

Moving on to the last point on the card, If it hadn't been for that visit then it's unlikely that I would now be so keen to learn more about Scottish history.

Points to note

- *a city I adore above all others*
A paraphrase of *favourite city*

- *do justice to something*
To describe or show something accurately. This is most often used in the negative to highlight that something is better than it appeared or was portrayed.

- *never before have I been so impressed*
A negative adverbial construction.

- *It was while I was exploring that I came across*
This narrative tense sequence also includes a phrasal verb. *To come across* something means to find it by chance.

- *off the beaten track*
An idiomatic phrase meaning hidden, remote, and rarely visited.

- *delve into*
A phrasal verb meaning to explore or examine something carefully to discover more information.

- *pleasing to the eye*
A phrase meaning particularly attractive.

• *If it hadn't been for that visit then it's unlikely that I would now ...*
A mixed conditional signifying a present result of a past condition.

Historical places

Historical places are a frequent cue card topic which is why I suggested when preparing your city answer that you should choose one which is of historical interest. If you have prepared Edinburgh as your city, then you can easily adapt it if you are asked to describe a historical place. Sometimes, however, you are asked about a building as in the following cue card:

> Talk about a historical building in your country or city that you know.
> You should say:
> what and where it is
> when was it built
> what is it known for
> and describe this historical building

Strategy

When choosing a historical building to talk about I would advise that you select one that is not only architecturally interesting but has also played a significant role in your country's history. It's possible that a building is of historical interest solely because of its design, such as a particularly original nineteenth-century house. There is far more to talk about, however, if the building is not only intrinsically interesting but has also been the setting for significant historical events. In my country, the nineteenth-century parliament building would be such an example.

One-minute notes

• a building of significant architectural and historical interest
• was built in the nineteenth century ... after a previous one had been destroyed
• pick out
• not only is it a major tourist attraction but it is also ...
• heated exchanges
• If you are interested in British politics I would ...

Sample answer

A building of significant architectural and historical interest in my country is the Palace of Westminster. It's also referred to as the Houses of Parliament and it is the seat of the British government. It's situated in a spectacular setting in the heart of London just by the River Thames and next to another iconic and historically important building, Westminster Abbey.

The present Palace of Westminster was built in the nineteenth century in the Gothic style after a previous one had been destroyed in a fire and the first thing that strikes you when you see the place is just how colossal it is. It's also extremely elaborate. There are a number of towers and turrets all festooned with flamboyant carvings. But if I had to pick out one feature to talk about it would be the clock tower. I would go as far as saying that it is probably the most famous clock in the world and a must-see for all tourists to London. The chime of its bell, called Big Ben, is instantly recognisable to all British people because it has been used to signal the start of television news programmes for many years.

What is it known for? Well, not only is it a major tourist attraction but it is also the place where the country's legislators meet to enact laws. It is sometimes referred to as the mother of parliaments and a symbol of democracy. The debating chambers have been the setting for some of the most important and dramatic speeches in British history. Often there are heated exchanges particularly when the Prime Minister has to answer questions from opposition politicians. This is televised and can often be highly entertaining. If you are interested in British politics, I would definitely recommend that you watch it.

Points to note

• *A building of significant architectural and historical interest*
A paraphrase of *historical building.*

• *iconic*
An adjective meaning *exemplary* or *emblematic*

• *was built in the nineteenth century ... after a previous one had been destroyed*
We can use passive as well as active forms in narrative tense sequences. Here we have a past simple passive followed by a past perfect passive.

• *colossal*
A better alternative to saying *very big.*

• *festooned with flamboyant carvings*
In addition to *colossal*, I have tried to use some less common vocabulary to describe the

palace such as *festooned* rather than *decorated*. *Flamboyant* is also a good alternative to *elaborate*.

• *pick out*
A phrasal verb meaning to choose one thing from a group of other things.

• *a must-see*
Something that is highly recommended.

• *not only is it a major tourist attraction but it is also ...*
A negative adverbial construction.

• *heated exchange*
An idiom for a lively and possibly angry argument.

• *If you are interested in British politics I would ...*
As always, it's a good plan to end on a conditional.

• You may note that I have not followed the cue card prompts in order. As a general rule, it is best that you do, that way you won't miss one, but sometimes you might feel it more appropriate to switch them. For this talk, I thought it better to describe the building first and finish with what it is used for. As long as you include everything it is not obligatory to follow the order.

By choosing a building that is historically and architecturally interesting and is also a tourist attraction I can recycle the material I have prepared for the following cue cards:

Describe a historical place that you know about.
You should say:
what the place is
where it is located
what is the historical significance of the place
and describe your experience of the place

Describe a tourist attraction that you enjoyed visiting
You should say:
where it was
who you went there with
what you did there
and explain what you enjoyed most about this place

Describe an important building in your country
You should say:
where it is
what it looks like
what it is used for
and explain why you think it is important

Describe an interesting historic place
You should say:
what is it
where it is located
what you can see there
and explain why this place is interesting

The natural world

Cue cards in this category broadly fall into one of two groups, places by water and landscapes such as parks and the countryside. For both, you are likely to be asked why you like these places and the key is to prepare vocabulary and phrases conveying peace, quiet, and relaxation. Also, it is a good idea to prepare places in your own country because sometimes this is specified.

For some reason watery places feature often in IELTS tests so we will start with this cue card:

Describe a river or sea you have visited
You should say:
where the river/sea is
what activities you did there
who was with you
and explain why you liked this particular place

Strategy

Again, for this cue card, I am going to choose not to answer each prompt in order. Quite clearly what the candidate is expected to do is focus on the river or sea. The people are quite incidental and a description of them would not be appropriate. I'm therefore going to mention them in passing near the beginning and use most of my talk to describe the landscape and our activities.

One-minute notes

- one of the most thrilling coastlines I have toured is
- rarely were we bored
- it was while we were swimming that we saw ...
- get the hang of it
- If I went back ... I would want to ...
- to try out

Sample answer

One of the most thrilling coastlines I have toured is that of the English region of Northumbria. This is in the far north east of the country facing the North Sea. It's just above the city of Newcastle and bordering Scotland. I went with a small group of friends a couple of years ago and we rented a quaint little cottage in a fishing village. There is certainly plenty to do in the region and rarely were we bored. The sea itself is almost always quite chilly, even in the height of the summer, so swimming is only for the brave and possibly foolhardy. But we all found it a most invigorating experience and after a while, we didn't notice the cold too much. You quickly get used to it.

It was while we were swimming on our first day that we saw people windsurfing. It was possible to hire the gear, so we decided to give it a go. It was my first time and I found it totally exhilarating. There's a steep learning curve before you get the hang of it and I did fall off the board a number of times but that was all part of the fun. Apparently, it's also a good place to go diving because there are submerged wrecks just beneath the waves. If I went back, it's definitely something I would want to try out.

But perhaps what I enjoyed the most was simply walking along the beaches. They are stunningly beautiful with miles of golden sand and, unlike in some coastal areas in the country, they are totally unspoilt. Virtually the only buildings to be seen are the dramatic ruins of castles. On one occasion we got up early and sat on the beach to see the sun rise above the horizon. Never before have I experienced something quite so beautiful. It was an unforgettable experience.

As you can probably gather, I thoroughly recommend the Northumbrian coast as a place to visit. You can't, unfortunately, guarantee the sun but if you want beautiful scenery and exciting water sports it's hard to beat.

Points to note

- *One of the most thrilling coastlines I have toured is ...*
I have replaced *sea* and *visit* with synonyms in my opening paraphrase.

- *rarely were we bored*
A negative adverb followed by verb inversion.

- *Foolhardy*
Foolhardy is a good word to use if you want to qualify *brave* and it means foolishly adventurous.

- *it was while we were swimming that we saw ...*
A narrative tense sequence.

- *invigorating*
When describing an energetic sport or activity the adjectives *invigorating* and *exhilarating* are useful to remember and are a good replacement for the too common *exciting*.

- *gear*
Gear is an example of a word that has a very precise meaning. In this context, it means special clothing and equipment used for a particular activity. For example, *I've decided to go rock climbing and I've bought all the gear.*

- *steep learning curve*
A phrase meaning that something is difficult to learn.

- *give something a go*
- *get the hang of*
I have included a couple of idioms both of which you can use if you are describing an activity that you tried for the first time. If you *give something a go* it simply means that you try it. And to *get the hang of* something means that you learn how to do it. The use of both is not restricted to sports, it can be almost any activity. For example, *I decided to have a go at learning Mandarin, but it was too difficult, and I never got the hang of it.*

- *If I went back, it's definitely something I would want to ...*
The second conditional construction.

- *try out*
A phrasal verb meaning to try something for the first time to see whether it's suitable or whether you like it.

- *never before have I ...*
This is a great negative adverbial inversion to use when talking about a first-time activity.

- *hard to beat*
This is a phrase that can replace the overused word *excellent*.

Here are some more water-themed cue cards:

> Describe a place near water (such as a river, lake, or ocean) that you enjoyed visiting.
> You should say:
> where this place was
> what you did at this place
> who you went there with
> and explain why you liked this place

> Describe a seaside place that you like to visit.
> You should say:
> where it is
> what you like to do there
> who you like to go with
> and explain why you like to go there

> Describe a popular place for swimming you know in our country.
> You should say:
> where it is
> what type of people go there
> when they usually visit this place
> and explain why it is a good place to go to

Let's move on from watery places to other areas of natural beauty. Here's a classic example of the genre:

> Describe an enjoyable place you have visited in the countryside.
> You should say:
> when you visited this place
> who was with you
> why this place was enjoyable
> and say if you would like to go back there in the future

Strategy

As always when preparing material in advance of the exam, if the cue card doesn't specify a country then it's best to use your own. I've also deliberately chosen a place which not only has attractive natural features but also some ancient man-made ones. That way, if the focus of the cue card had been slightly different and asked about a historical landscape, I could easily have adapted the material.

One-minute notes

- a delightful rural landscape I saw
- had heard of a ... and suggested that we ...
- not often do you find
- cheek by jowl
- find out
- If you ever ..., I would definitely recommend that you ...

Sample answer

A delightful rural landscape I saw recently is a place called Sutton Park. I have a friend who has moved to the city of Birmingham because he has a new job there and he invited me to stay with him for the weekend. To be honest with you I find the city neither interesting nor attractive and we quickly exhausted what few delights it has to offer the weekend tourist. But fortunately, my friend had heard of a large urban park on the outskirts of the city and suggested that we investigate.

It's only a relatively short train or bus ride from the bustling city centre but it's like being transported into a different world. What I found particularly enjoyable and astonishing for that matter, was the variety of different natural landscapes in a relatively small area. Not often do you find lakes and streams cheek by jowl with heathland, marshes, and woods. It's like a microcosm of the whole English countryside.

What I really appreciated was a visitor centre near the entrance. The staff were very knowledgeable and when they found out that I was interested in ancient history they gave me a map and pointed out a prehistoric well and the remains of a Roman road we could discover. So off we went to explore. I was absolutely in my element and it wasn't until the light started to fade that we decided to call it a day and go home.

I definitely want to go back again in the future. I've looked up Sutton Park on the internet and discovered that there is a plethora of interesting things to see that we missed the first time around - the earthworks of a prehistoric encampment, for example, are something that I am very eager to explore. If you ever find yourself in Birmingham, I recommend that you head out of the city centre and visit Sutton Park.

Points to note

- *A delightful rural landscape I saw*
A paraphrase of *enjoyable place in the countryside*.

• *we exhausted what few delights*
You may want to convey the idea that a particular place is not very interesting so that you can contrast it with another place that is. A good way of doing this using less common vocabulary is, *we exhausted what few delights it has to offer*. This is a good way of saying that a place didn't have many interesting things to see.

• *He had heard of a large urban park ... and suggested that we investigate.*
Past perfect followed by past simple to indicate a sequence of events.

• *Not often do you find*
A negative adverb followed by the inverted verb. You can also use *seldom* and *rarely*.

• *Cheek by jowl*
An idiom that you can use to indicate that things are close to each other in an unexpected or surprising way.

• *microcosm*
A microcosm is a small place that has the characteristics of something much larger. For example, *my city is wonderfully multicultural. It feels like a microcosm of the whole continent.*

• *find out* and *point out*
I've included a couple of common phrasal verbs, *to find out* meaning discover and *point out* meaning to show where something is.

• *in my element*
A great idiom to use to say that you are doing something that you find enjoyable and that you do well is, *I am in my element.*

• *To call it a day*
An idiom meaning that you stopped doing something either temporarily or permanently.

• *look up*
A common phrasal verb meaning to find information about something by looking in a book or on the internet.

• A *plethora*
A plethora of something is a large amount.

• *If you ever ..., I would definitely recommend that you ...*
My recommended conditional ending when you think you are near to your two minutes and have nothing more to say.

There are lots of possible variations on the countryside/natural landscape theme. Here are a few:

> Talk about a picnic spot/recreational public spot that you like.
> You should say:
> what it is and where it is located
> what attractive things are there for visitors
> what types of people like to go there
> and explain why you enjoy visiting this place

> Talk about a place of natural beauty that you like to visit.
> You should say:
> what and where it is
> why you like to visit
> when you like to visit
> and explain why this place is worth visiting

> Describe a garden or park you enjoyed visiting.
> You should say:
> where it was
> what it looked like
> what people were doing there
> and explain why you liked it

Please remember that total honesty and accuracy is not essential. Sutton Park, as I have described above, is on the edge of an urban area and not actually in it. But with a minor tweak, I could use it for the following cue card. The examiner will not question my geographical accuracy.

> Describe your favourite park in your city.
> You should say:
> where it is
> what you can see and do there
> how frequently you go there
> and explain why this is your favourite park

Occasionally cue cards ask you to describe peaceful, relaxing, or tranquil places without specifically mentioning the countryside or any natural features. Quite clearly the material you have prepared for the natural world can be reused.

Talk about a peaceful place that you like.
You should say:
where the place is
what it looks like
how you came to know about this place
and explain why you like this place

Places you visit as part of your regular routine

This is obviously a very broad category and therefore a little difficult to prepare for. The opportunities for directly reusing material are fewer. However, there are a couple of useful things to do in advance. One is to prepare some vocabulary to describe the interiors of rooms and buildings. The other is to prepare ways to compare and contrast places. Many of the cue cards in this category ask you about favourite venues that you visit such as shops, cafes, restaurants, libraries, etc. You will find it very useful to be able to say why you like one such place in preference to another.

Let's start with the first and an example of an interior in your home.

Describe your study room.
You should say:
what it looks like
what furniture it contains
how much time you spend in this room
and give details of an ideal study room

Strategy

I should start by saying that this card does not actually specify that the study room should be in your own home. However, you are sometimes asked to describe a favourite room in your house or one that you like to spend time in. I'm therefore going to talk about a study room in my own home in the hope that I could reuse the material.

My usual advice for part two is to start with a paraphrase and finish with a conditional. Here, however, I have spotted a good opportunity to start with a conditional. If you are asked to describe something that you own or belongs to you, then sometimes an option is to start by saying that if you had more money you would probably get a bigger or better thing, but in the meantime, you will talk about you about what you have. I've saved my paraphrase for the last line of the prompt.

One-minute notes

- If I had more money I would
- make do
- a riot of colour.
- the perfect place to read and think
- rarely am I disturbed
- when we were moving in she chose

Sample answer

If I had more money, I would definitely buy a larger house because it is my dream to have a dedicated study lined with books. As it is, I have to make do with my bedroom. Fortunately, it is sufficiently large for me to have a desk in one corner. As for its appearance, to be honest, I've never really been into interior decoration so it's nothing special to look at. You could say that it's quite minimalistic with just the basic furnishings that you would expect to find in a bedroom - a bed, wardrobe, and chest of drawers. I'm not keen on patterns so I chose soft furnishings like the bedding, curtains, and rug in plain muted tones. And the walls are painted white so it's hardly a riot of colour.

So it's probably fair to say that it's not a room to everybody's taste but what I do find is that it is very conducive to study which is good because just recently I've been preparing hard for this exam, at least three or four hours a day. And then, when you factor in the time that I sleep, I'm spending the best part of a dozen hours in there.

As for the perfect place to read and think, the key ingredient for me is a lack of distractions. I've already indicated that the decor in my room is hardly likely to interfere with my concentration but something that's also important to me is peace and quiet. My bedroom is at the rear of my house overlooking a garden. It's incredibly tranquil and rarely am I disturbed by noise. My sister, on the other hand, has her bedroom at the front overlooking the street. When we were moving in she chose the room with a more interesting view, but I would find the noise of the traffic and people passing by a huge distraction.

Points to note

- *If I had more money I would ...*
A conditional phrase that can be used in many IELTS answers, not just part two.

- *dedicated*
If something is *dedicated* then it is exclusively allocated to or intended for a particular purpose. My current study space is not a dedicated study because I also have to sleep in

the room. Note the slightly different meaning of *dedicated* when used to describe a person. A *dedicated* doctor is one who is devoted to his job

• *as it is*
The phrase *as it is* is used when you want to describe a situation that actually exists rather than one which you expected, needed, or would prefer. For example, *I really need a new car but as it is I'll have to keep my old one for a little longer*

• *make do*
To do as well as you can with what you have. The implication is that ideally, you would like something more or better.

• *be into something*
To be interested in or enthusiastic about something.

• *to my taste*
To my taste means the same as *to my liking*. It doesn't have to be connected to tastes in food but can be almost anything. For example, *opera is not really to my taste. I much prefer jazz.*

• *a riot of colour*
an idiom meaning very bright and colourful.

• *factor in*
A phrasal verb meaning to take something into consideration.

• *the best part of*
A phrase meaning *most of*.

• *the perfect place to read and think*
A paraphrase for an *ideal study room*.

• *peace and quiet*
A very common collocation. When the two words are together they are always in this order.

• *rarely am I disturbed*
A negative adverbial construction.

• *when we were moving in, she chose ...*
narrative sequence of past continuous followed by past simple.

Here are some variations on the theme of rooms. As always, pay attention to the main verb tense. You may, as in the second sample below, be asked about a room from your past.

> Describe your favourite room.
> You should say:
> what the room is
> what furniture it contains
> what you do in it
> and explain why it is your favourite room

> Describe a room for you stayed for a long period.
> You should say:
> what room it was
> what you did there
> why you spent so much time there
> and describe the memories you have regarding this room

> Describe a room that you like.
> You should say:
> which room it is
> what makes this room special
> what it looks like
> and explain how you feel when you are in this room

Let's now move on from your home to places in your town or city that you often visit. Restaurants and cafes make regular appearances in all three parts of the speaking test and here's a typical example from part two.

> Describe your favourite restaurant.
> You should say:
> where it is
> what it looks like inside and outside
> what kinds of food they serve
> and explain what makes this restaurant so special

Strategy

You don't usually get much choice about which room in your home you sleep in, but this is not the case for places like restaurants. My strategy for these cue cards is to explain why I like such venues by comparing and contrasting them to the alternatives. There are a number of phrases and devices you can use which will increase your grammatical range score and this strategy will also give your talk structure, making it more fluent and coherent.

One-minute notes

- the number one place to eat out
- I first came across it by accident when I was exploring
- If you enjoy Italian food, I'm sure you would love ...
- made from scratch
- rarely do they know your name.

Sample answer

For me, the number one place to eat out in this city is a place run by a chef called Luigi. His eponymous restaurant is extremely popular, and deservedly so. The actual building is a little off the beaten track and I first came across it by accident when I was exploring some of the little side streets away from the main shopping area. It's actually a very unassuming place from the outside and you could easily walk by without realising that it is a restaurant. And the interior is also not particularly fancy or flamboyant. There are about half a dozen small tables and a few photographs of streets in Naples hanging on the walls. These give the only indication of the type of cuisine to expect.

But it is the food and the service that make me, and lots of other regulars, return time after time. It's quite a basic menu, just a few pizza and pasta dishes but all the ones I have tried are absolutely delicious. If you enjoy Italian food, I'm sure you would love the place.

There are a lot of chain Italian restaurants in the city but what they do is quite formulaic. I'm sure they just buy pre-prepared dishes in bulk and then reheat them. Luigi's, on the other hand, is truly authentic. He buys fresh ingredients from the market early every morning and the menu changes according to what he finds available. Every dish is made from scratch. And although the service in the chain places is okay, it's hardly personal. I'm just one of a large number of customers that evening and rarely do they know your name.

This is in stark contrast to Luigi and his staff who take the time to get to know your individual likes and dislikes. He knows that I love basil, for example, and there is always a big sprig of it on top of my pasta dish. It's little things like that that make this restaurant so special to me and to others.

Points to note

• *For me, the number one place to eat out*
A paraphrase of *favourite restaurant.*

• *eponymous*
The restaurant I describe is loosely based on a real place, but I have changed a few details so that I can incorporate some less common vocabulary and phrases. It isn't, for example, called Luigi's but renaming it enables me to use the word *eponymous,* an adjective meaning a place named after a person

• *I first came across it by accident when I was exploring*
A narrative sequence of past simple with past continuous. This particular phrase is very useful when you are describing how you first found a place. Not only is it a narrative tense sequence but it also contains the phrasal verb to *come across,* meaning to find by chance.

• *unassuming* and *flamboyant*
Unassuming is a good word to describe either a place or person, meaning unpretentious and modest. *Flamboyant* is almost the opposite and again can be used to describe either a place or a person. It means ostentatious or exuberant.

• *time after time*
an idiom meaning repeatedly.

• *If you enjoy Italian food, I'm sure you would love the place*
Another useful conditional sentence you can adapt for many part two responses.

• *Formulaic*
Formulaic simply means something constructed or made according to a formula. But it has slightly negative connotations and is useful for describing things that are not particularly original and are too similar to others.

• *made from scratch*
If you *make something from scratch* it means that you start from the beginning with basic ingredients. It doesn't just refer to food, a good craftsman should be able to make a wardrobe from scratch for example.

• *rarely do they know your name*
A negative adverbial structure.

• *stark contrast*

This is a collocation meaning that something is very different from something else.

Here are some other familiar place cue cards where you can display your ability to describe contrast.

Describe a hotel you have stayed in.
You should say:
where the hotel is
why you stayed in that particular hotel
what the interior of the hotel was like
and explain what makes the hotel special

Describe a cafe that you like to visit
You should say:
where it is
how often you go there
when you usually go there
and explain why you like to visit this cafe

Describe a shop or store that you often go to
You should say:
where it is
what types of people go there
what types of goods are sold there
and explain why you go there and what you like about it

And finally, for this section let's look at what I sometimes call hypothetical place cue cards. As I have said before you always need to look at the key tense in the first prompt on the card. It's particularly important for place cue cards because one word - *would* - totally changes the meaning. Look at the following:

Describe a foreign country that you would like to visit
You should say:
where it is
how you know about this country
what this country is like
and explain why you would like to visit this country

Quite clearly the intention is that you should talk about a country that you haven't been to. The problem, of course, is that if you haven't been to a place then you are unlikely to know very much about it. The solution is to describe a foreign country that you have visited in the past and make a few adjustments, primarily verb tenses and the addition of a few phrases to indicate that you are not speaking from first-hand experience.

Here's my sample answer to the card above but using the material from my Italy answer at the beginning of this chapter.

I should like to tell you about Italy, a country in southern Europe in the heart of the Mediterranean Sea. I've seen many films set in Italy and also a number of travel programmes about the place, but I mainly know about it from my uncle. He and his family visited last year, and he's told me that it's a fascinating and exceptionally beautiful country.

After they had flown into Rome, they hired a car so that they could tour around the major cities. He's advised me that this is not such a great idea as it might seem. He only had a week's holiday and a couple of days in each place was nothing like enough. He said that they barely scratched the surface of what each city had to offer. I understand that you could easily spend a month in Rome and still keep finding new things to see.

Anyway, on their visit to the capital, they did a lightning tour of the major monuments such as the Coliseum and St Peter's before heading off for Florence and Milan. Those places sound amazing and I've come to the conclusion that, for me, Italy is probably the perfect country to visit. First, if you're interested in art, I have been led to believe that it's an absolute cultural haven with probably the finest Renaissance paintings and sculptures in the world. Second, you have a wide variety of landscapes from mountains and lakes to miles of breathtaking coastline. And last, but not least, is the food. Italian cuisine is renown throughout the world and rightly so with each region having interesting and delicious specialities

In short, it's a country that would appear to have something for everyone and I'm extremely eager to visit at the earliest opportunity.

The strategy I have used is to tell the story of my visit but pretending that it was my uncle, rather than me, who went. That enables me to explain how I know about the country. There are also a number of useful little phrases which you can use to show that your knowledge of a place is not from personal experience:

- *I have been led to believe that Italy is exceptionally beautiful.*

- *I understand that Italy is exceptionally beautiful.*

- *Italy is supposed to be exceptionally beautiful.*

- *It's common knowledge that Italy is exceptionally beautiful.*

Here are some more hypothetical place cue cards:

Describe a foreign country you have never been to.
You should say:
where the country is
when you will go there
why you would like to go there
and explain why you think this is a good country to visit

Describe a place where you would like to go.
You should say:
where the place is
how you would get there
what it looks like
and explain why you would like to visit this place

Describe a journey that you would like to make.
You should say:
where you would travel to
what type of transport you would choose
what the purpose of our journey would be
and give details of your plan of the journey

THINGS

By *things* I mean physical objects that you can touch and intangible ones such as films or pieces of music. You might think that this would be a difficult category to prepare for because there are millions of different objects. In reality, however, most of the cue cards in this category allow you to choose the actual item. The card merely restricts you to a category and these, by and large, are limited to:

- Things that you own and have a special meaning

- Gifts and presents either given by you or to you

- Beautiful objects such as artworks you have seen in a museum or gallery

- Photographs

- Modern technology

- Useful domestic appliances

- Items of clothing

- Things produced in your country

- Intangibles

Special things

A special thing is something that is distinctive and possibly unique. Your smartphone might be an object you consider important and couldn't live without, but most people have one and yours is unlikely to be much different from anybody else's. Instead, try to think of an old object that has sentimental rather than monetary value, something that perhaps evokes memories of previous generations of your family.

In the introduction to part two, we looked at an example of a special things cue card and the sample answer of an old watch. Here's a variation on that card:

Describe an antique or other old object that your family has kept for a long time.
You should say:
what it is
how your family first got this thing
how long your family has kept it
and explain why this object is important to your family

Strategy

In practice sessions with my students, this card has caused some difficulties because they couldn't think of such an object. Not all families want to keep such things, so you might need to be inventive. One student came up with what I thought was an excellent response because she remembered a cultural family tradition that was common in her country. Her own family didn't keep up this tradition but, like the best IELTS students, she could be very creative when necessary. I have remodelled her answer, with some amendments, below.

One-minute notes

- my forebears have treasured for generations
- not very much to look at
- passed down
- after a child had been born the father would record
- seldom did all the children
- if I am fortunate, I would love to see

Sample answer

An heirloom that my forebears have treasured for generations is a bible. It's likely that members of my extended family own a number of bibles but this one is especially important to us. It's not very much to look at and, from the cover, it looks much like any old small leather-bound volume. Engraved on the spine in small gold letters are the words 'family bible' but these are quite faded now so it's not immediately obvious what type of book it is.

This particular bible dates from the early nineteenth century and was probably originally bought in a shop. There's no sure way of knowing now, but what I do know is that the first owner was one of my ancestors and it has subsequently been passed down to the eldest sons of the family. My grandfather currently looks after it. He often emphasises the fact that he doesn't own it, he's merely the custodian for future generations.

The reason why it is so important to us is that it was a common tradition in the nineteenth century to write the details and dates of significant family events on the blank pages inside the front cover. So, after a child had been born the father would record the name and date. It was similar for marriages and deaths. I just find it absolutely fascinating and quite poignant. I like to conjure up images of what the family weddings must have been like all those years ago and the joy at each new birth.

But what I find particularly touching, in fact almost heartbreaking, are the records of the deaths. Seldom did all the children in a family survive into adulthood and there are a number of instances recorded of a baby being born but tragically dying a few days later.

My family continues to use the book as originally intended. My birth is noted in it and one day, if I am fortunate, my children's names will be written there too. For me, the bible is an object beyond value.

Points to note

• *an heirloom that my forebears have treasured for generations*
This paraphrases *an antique or other old object that your family has kept for a long time.*
Treasure is most commonly used as a noun, particularly in the collocation *a treasured possession*, but it can be useful as a verb. It means to keep something that you like very much and is important to you.

• *not very much to look at*
Not much to look at means not physically attractive. It is often followed by *but* and is a good construction to use when showing a contrast. For example, *my old car is not much to look at but it's incredibly reliable and has never broken down.*

• *not immediately obvious*
This and the opposite, *immediately obvious,* are common collocations that native speakers use often. If something is *not immediately obvious* it is not able to be seen or understood easily.

• *passed down*
The phrasal verb *passed down* denotes something handed from one generation to the next.

• *look after*
This phrasal verb is most commonly used in connection with people, especially children. It may also be used with objects and it means to guard and protect.

• *after a child had been born the father would record*
Past perfect followed by past simple to show a sequence of events.

• *Conjure up*

This is a phrasal verb that has a couple of meanings. In the passage above it means to bring a feeling or a picture to your mind. It can also mean to produce or make something very quickly in a way that is surprising. For example, *my relatives arrived unexpectedly, and I had to conjure up a meal from the few things I had in the fridge.*

• *poignant*

If something is *poignant* it evokes memories of sadness or regret.

• *seldom did all the children*

A negative adverbial construction.

• *if I am fortunate, my children's names will be written*

A first conditional with the result clause in the future simple passive.

Here is a cue card where you could reuse your prepared material with minor modifications:

> Describe a thing which you possess, and which is important to you.
> You should say:
> what it is and how you obtained it
> what is special about it
> whether you would ever give it to somebody else
> and explain why it is important to you

And here are a couple of variations on the theme of special things for you to think about:

> Describe something special you brought home from a holiday.
> You should say:
> what it was
> when and where you went on this holiday
> what you did with it after you brought it home
> and explain why you thought it was special

Describe something special that you saved money to buy.
You should say:
what it was
how long it took you to save the money
why you wanted to buy this thing
and explain how you felt when you bought it

Gifts and presents

There is some overlap between this category and the previous one. Gifts, after all, are usually special in some way. However, because gift-themed cue cards are quite common, I have dealt with them separately.

Present giving is, of course, a two-way process. Here is a card where you are the recipient.

Describe a gift that you have received that was important to you.
You should say:
what it is
who gave it to you and for what occasion
how you use it
and explain why it is important to you

Strategy

There is usually plenty to talk about with gift-themed questions and my students don't usually have too many problems with them. Not only do you have the object itself but also the relationship between the donor and recipient, and the occasion. Ideally, you should choose objects and occasions of significance. A box of chocolates on your birthday doesn't give you much to talk about. I could, of course, reuse the heirloom watch given to me by my father on my birthday but I'm going to use the example of a wedding present.

One-minute notes

• one of the most special presents I have ever received
• when we were considering ... we both immediately thought ...
• think twice
• reflect on

- if we had married in …, they wouldn't have had …
- rarely do I look at it

Sample answer

One of the most special presents I have ever received was for my wedding. I met my wife when we were both students at university and we got married last summer. When we were considering possible wedding venues, we both immediately thought of the chapel on the campus. It's a picturesque old building and we are both friends with the chaplain, so we didn't really need to think twice.

After we had decided on the location there were obviously lots of other things we needed to reflect on and the issue of presents was one of the more problematic. Neither of us wanted our family to feel obliged to fork out lots of money on gifts because most faced long journeys to get there. If we had married in either of our hometowns, they wouldn't have had travelling and hotel expenses. In the end, we placed at a department store a list of things that we really needed, but most were quite low-cost items like cutlery and crockery.

However, my sister decided to get us something really special. I have always been very close to her and we share many of the same likes and dislikes. What she did was to surreptitiously obtain a photograph of the chapel and she commissioned a talented artist that she knew to reproduce it in a watercolour.

It really is exquisite, and it occupies pride of place over the fireplace in our living room. It complements the decor of the place perfectly. And it's unique, a genuinely original work of art and that makes it quite special. But it's not because it looks beautiful that I love it so much, it's because it means so much to both of us. Rarely do I look at it without thinking of our university days and, of course, the wedding. It brings back so many happy memories.

Points to note

- *One of the most special presents I have ever received*
A paraphrase of *a gift that you have received that was important to you.*

- *When we were considering possible wedding venues, we both immediately thought …*
I have used two narrative tense structures in this story. Past continuous plus past simple in the sentence, *When we were considering possible wedding venues we both immediately thought of the chapel.* There is also past simple plus past perfect in, *After we had decided on the location there were obviously lots of other things we needed to reflect on.*

- *to think twice*
An idiom meaning to think seriously about whether you really want to do something

before doing it. It's often used in the negative form, for example, *I didn't have to think twice* indicating that the decision was easy to make.

• *reflect on*
A phrasal verb meaning to consider carefully.

• *fork out*
The phrasal verb *fork out* means to pay for something unwillingly.

• *If we had married in either of our hometowns, they wouldn't have had travelling and hotel expenses*
A third conditional.

• *close to*
The idiomatic phrase *close to* somebody means that you have a particularly deep and meaningful relationship.

• *surreptitiously*
If you do something surreptitiously it means that you do it secretively or in a way that avoids attention.

• *exquisite*
I have used a couple of the less common adjectives to replace *beautiful* here, *picturesque* to indicate that the chapel is quaint and charming, and *exquisite* meaning exceptionally fine.

• *Rarely do I look at it*
A negative adverbial structure.

• *bring back*
The phrasal verb *bring back*, meaning to remind you of something, often collocates with the word memories. Photographs and pieces of music, in particular, can often bring back happy memories.

Instead of being asked about a present you have received, you may be asked about one you have given. One easy way of dealing with this is to switch the donor and recipient in your prepared material. So for the following cue card, you could talk about the special painting you gave to your sister for her wedding.

Talk about a gift that you gave to someone recently.
You should say:
what the gift was
who you gave it to
how you felt about it
and explain why you chose this gift

Here are a couple more gift cue cards to consider:

Describe a present you received as a child.
You should say:
what the present was
who gave it to you
how you used this present
and explain how you felt when you got this present

Describe the best gift you have received.
You should say:
what the gift was
who gave it to you
when you received it
and explain why it was such a good gift

Works of Art

It is only rarely that you are asked to talk about a specific type of artwork, such as a painting or sculpture. You will usually be able to choose. Sometimes the card indicates that the work of art should be one that you have seen in a museum or gallery as in this example:

Describe a statue or other work of art that you have seen.
You should say:
where you saw it
when you saw it
what it looked like
and explain your understanding of what this work of art means or represents

Strategy

What actually constitutes a work of art is debatable but an IELTS part two answer is not the place for controversial theories. Play it safe and choose a traditional sculpture or painting. I would also choose an object that is housed in a museum or gallery because this type of location is sometimes specified.

The majority of the cue cards in this category ask you about objects that you personally like or find beautiful. The one above is unusual because it doesn't. There is absolutely no reason why you shouldn't choose something you did enjoy looking at, and this is probably the easiest and safest option. However another strategy, if you feel confident enough to do it, is to opt for an object which you don't particularly like but recognise is good. This potentially gives more scope for increasing your fluency and coherence score because you will be using more complex reasoning skills. My sample answer below is an example of this.

One-minute notes

- I first set eyes on the notable painting …
- it was when we were visiting …
- thinking back
- only much later did I get the chance
- bucket list
- I would definitely recommend that you should … if you visit …

Sample answer

I first set eyes on the notable painting, 'Sunflowers' by the Dutch artist Vincent Van Gogh some years ago. It was when we were visiting the National Gallery in London on a school outing. We were being taken on a guided tour of some of the best-known works of art in the collection and our guide told us that it was one of the most famous and important paintings in the world.

As for a description, well it's basically a still life of a bunch of sunflowers in a simple pot. Some of the individual flowers look quite fresh but a few are beginning to droop. The flowers themselves, unsurprisingly perhaps, are yellow but the background, just a plain wall is also in a muted shade of the same colour. Even the pot and table that it stands on are painted in yellow hues.

Our guide told us that the flowers were symbols, they represented light and joy and the painting is all about hope and optimism. Thinking back, I wasn't overly impressed. To my untrained eye it didn't look skilfully painted, the surface of the table wasn't even flat.

Only much later did I get the chance to re-evaluate my original opinions when I revisited the gallery as an adult. I think I appreciate it a little better now, and I do recognise why it is highly regarded by experts. Part of the problem for me, I think, is that the image is ubiquitous. It's almost a visual cliché and seems to be everywhere from T towels to shower curtains. But I suppose it's one of those bucket list paintings like the Mona Lisa and I would definitely recommend that you should see Van Gogh's sunflowers if you visit the National Gallery.

Points to note

• *I first set eyes on the notable painting*
A paraphrase of *a work of art that you have seen.*
The idiom *to set eyes on* means to see something or somebody, usually for the first time.

• *it was when we were visiting …*
The first part of my response is a story of a visit to a gallery and I have twice used the narrative tense structure of past continuous plus past simple. In the first, the continuous verb is in the active mode - *It was when we were visiting the gallery on a school outing.* For variation I have then used the past continuous in the passive form followed by past simple - *We were being taken on a guided tour … and our guide told us…*

• *still life*
A still life is a work of art depicting inanimate and ordinary objects.

• *thinking back*
The phrasal verb to *think back* is to consider something from the past. Starting a sentence with *thinking back* is a useful device in IELTS part two.

• *untrained eye*
If you use an *untrained eye* it means that you have little knowledge of a particular subject.

• *only much later did I get the chance*
Only later did I … is an inversion with negative adverbial easily incorporated into many part two talks.

• *cliché*
The word *cliché* is usually associated with the written or spoken word and it means a phrase or opinion that is overused and lacking originality. It is also possible to have a visual *cliché* and it is one which is seen so often that it has lost its original meaning.

• *ubiquitous*
If something is ubiquitous then it is seen everywhere.

- *bucket list*

A *bucket list* is an idiom of recent origin and it signifies a list of things you want to see or do during your lifetime.

- *I would definitely recommend that you should … if you visit …*

There is no reason why you shouldn't directly address the examiner in part two. The best place to do this is at the end of your talk using a conditional and the best opportunity is if you are talking about something that the examiner might not have seen or experienced. For example, *if you were to visit my city I would definitely recommend that you visit the museum.*

Here are some works of art cue card variations:

> Describe an object or work of art you find particularly beautiful.
> You should say:
> where the artwork/object is
> how it was made
> what it shows/looks like
> and explain why you find it particularly beautiful

> Talk about a painting you would like to have in our home.
> You should say:
> what it is
> how you know about it
> how much it would cost you
> and explain why you would want to have it in your home

Photographs

In this category, you will be asked to describe a photograph that you like because it is attractive and appealing in some way or because it has a special significance for you. Often you will be able to talk about both aspects as in the following cue card:

> Describe one of your favourite photographs.
> You should say:
> when the photograph was taken
> what it looks like
> what significant memory you have regarding this photograph
> and explain why it is one of your favourite photographs

Strategy

Photographs evoke memories for a number of reasons. It could be because of the occasion when the picture was taken, for example, a wedding, or because of the people in it. It could, of course, be both of these. In addition, a photograph could bring back memories because of where you saw it. It might have hung on the wall in the house of your favourite grandmother.

Photographs can also be especially poignant because they depict people no longer living. They are often your only link to previous generations of your family. And photographs can be beautiful objects in themselves irrespective of what they depict.

The cue card above gives you a wonderful opportunity to combine all of these elements into an appealing story.

One-minute notes

- Sunday best
- only later when I was older did I understand ...
- I still find the image as compelling ...
- having done a little detective work I discovered ...
- worked out
- It would be so much easier if I had listened more carefully to my grandmother.

Sample answer

When I was very young I used to be fascinated by an ancient photograph that hung on the wall of my grandmother's living room. It's in faded sepia tones and depicts a group of people standing in front of a very grand mansion. I think it was the clothes that interested me the most. The people in the foreground are wearing their Sunday best, whereas those at the back are in a variety of uniforms. Only later when I was older did I understand what the picture actually depicted. It is the household of a large country house and the people in the most prominent positions are the immediate family of the owner, presumably a wealthy and important man. The men and women in the background are his servants, the maids, butlers, and cooks.

My grandmother explained that one of the young men standing at the back worked in the stables looking after the owner's horses and carriages and he was one of her ancestors. She knew exactly what the relationship was, he was something like a great uncle, and she also remembered the name of the house. Regrettably, I didn't note down these essential details and my mother no longer recalls them.

My grandmother, unfortunately, is no longer with us and the photograph now hangs in my mother's home. I still find the image as compelling as I did when I was a child. For one thing, it's actually a rather attractive object in its own right, irrespective of the family links. But it's that direct connection from me to the distant past that I find so enthralling and I often wonder what that young man's life was like. I just wish I knew what his name was.

Having done a little detective work I discovered that the photograph was taken in the latter half of the nineteenth century. I've also worked out which house it is so I'm getting a little closer to knowing who he was. It would be so much easier if I had listened more carefully to my grandmother.

Points to note

• *faded sepia tones*
Sepia is a reddish-brown colour often associated with very old photographs.

• *mansion*
A large impressive house.

• *Sunday best*
An idiom meaning your best clothes worn on special occasions.

• *only later when I was older did I understand ...*
A negative adverbial construction.

• *I still find the image as compelling ...*
Although I recommend starting your talk with a paraphrase of the first line of the prompt, you don't always have to do this. In this instance, I decided instead to launch into my story. It's later that I have paraphrased *favourite photograph* with *compelling image.*
Launch into, incidentally, is a phrasal verb meaning to begin something enthusiastically.

• *enthralling*
An excellent alternative to *very interesting.*

• *having done a little detective work I discovered ...*
A sequence of events described using a perfect participle followed by a past simple.

• *work out*
This phrasal verb has a number of meanings. It can mean to exercise in a gym but here it means to find the solution to something.

• *It would be so much easier if I had listened more carefully to my grandmother.*
A mixed conditional signifying the present result of a past condition.

Similar cue cards

> Describe an old photograph that you like.
> You should say:
> who took the photograph
> when it was taken
> where it was taken
> and explain why you like it

> Describe a photograph that you remember.
> You should say:
> when it was taken
> who took it
> what is in the photograph
> and explain why you remember this photograph

Modern Technology

Even if you don't get a technology cue card it's possible that you will be asked about the subject in either part one or part three. It's definitely worth thinking about the computers, smartphones, eBook readers, etc. that you own or use. Consider not only suitable vocabulary but also the advantages and disadvantages of such technology.

Here is a standard cue card in this category:

> Describe an item of modern technology that you own.
> You should say:
> what it is
> what you use it for
> how long you have owned it
> and explain why it is important to you.

Strategy

Inevitably some cue cards are considerably more popular with students during practice sessions than others. The ones that tend to be favoured are those where the subject matter is familiar, as it is in this one. Everybody I have met who has been preparing for the exam has owned at least one piece of modern technology. Given the choice between talking about their smartphone or about an antique object kept by their family for a long time, nine times out of ten they will choose the former.

The problem, however, is that the 'easy' cue cards are often not the ones that give you the greatest scope for exhibiting your fluency and coherence skills and your grammatical range. You can tell a good story about a family antique using a variety of narrative tenses and idioms. It is less easy to do this when you are talking about your mobile phone.

So beware of the 'easy' subject. A list of the features of your phone won't get you a high grade. Instead, use your minute to think of a story that incorporates the four prompts, and which will also enable you to display a coherent narrative.

One-minute notes

- a state-of-the-art gadget that I possess
- come out
- rarely am I satisfied
- when all is said and done
- returns to normal after you have been exercising
- if the smartwatch detects any abnormalities, it will alert you

Sample answer

A state-of-the-art gadget that I possess and find extremely useful is my smartwatch. I've always been an early adopter of new technology and so it was inevitable, I suppose, that I would get one as soon as they came out a few years ago. Rarely am I satisfied with outdated devices, so I'm actually already on my third iteration of the same model.

Some of my friends think that smartwatches are nothing more than expensive toys for adults and I even read somewhere that they provide a solution to non-existent problems. I can appreciate why people think this way because, when all is said and done, a smartwatch doesn't appear to do very much more than a smartphone. I use mine primarily to note the time, look at appointments in the calendar, check off boxes in my to-do list, and read incoming text messages. All of those you can do on the phone.

And there are, of course, drawbacks. The screen on the watch is too small for anything but basic information so if I need to look something up on the internet or read the latest news then out comes the smartphone. It might not be immediately apparent therefore why anybody would want to pay a few hundred pounds for the watch.

But I do have a reason and it's because of what I consider to be the device's killer app. It has a heart rate sensor linked to an application that monitors what the beat is throughout the day.

And because the watch also has a motion sensor it knows whether you are sitting, walking briskly, or doing a heavy workout.

It is important to know how quickly your heart rate returns to normal after you have been exercising and I do check when I'm at the gym. There's a history of heart problems in my family so I like to keep tabs on these things. If the smartwatch detects any abnormalities, it will alert you and potentially that could have lifesaving consequences. For me, that's an important enough reason for having one.

Points to note

• *A state-of-the-art gadget that I possess*
A paraphrase of *an item of modern technology that you own.*
State-of-the-art means ultra-modern and using the latest technology.
A gadget is a small mechanical or electronic device, which is ingenious or novel.

• *early adopter*
An early adopter is someone who is eager to buy the latest products or services, usually before other people do so.

• *come out*
The phrasal verb *to come out* has a number of different meanings. In the context above it means when something becomes available, usually for the first time. For example, *I always like to see the latest Hollywood blockbuster films as soon as they come out.*

• *iteration*
An iteration is a new version of a piece of computer hardware or software.

• *when all is said and done*
The idiomatic phrase, *when all is said and done,* is an alternative way of saying when everything is taken into account.

• *check off*
To *check off* is a phrasal verb meaning to make a mark next to an item on a list to show that you have dealt with it. The phrasal verb to *tick off* has the same meaning.

• *immediately apparent*
We have already seen the collocation phrase *not immediately obvious.* Not *immediately apparent* means the same.

• *killer app*
A *killer app* is a relatively new and informal noun. It means a computer application that is

so useful or popular that people are inclined to purchase the hardware just for that feature.

• *It is important to know how quickly your heart rate returns to normal after you have been exercising*
In this sentence, I have used the tense sequence of past simple plus present perfect continuous to describe a habitual action that takes place over an extended period of time followed by a single action.

• *so I like to keep tabs*
If you *keep tabs on something* it means you monitor it carefully. You can also keep tabs on people as in, *my boss likes to keep tabs on people all the time because he doesn't trust them to do their jobs properly.*

• *If the smartwatch detects any abnormalities, it will alert ...*
A first conditional.

Similar cue cards

Sometimes the card will specify that you should talk about a technological item as in this example:

> **Describe a piece of electronic equipment that you find useful.**
> **You should say:**
> **what it is**
> **how you learned to use it**
> **how long you have had it**
> **and explain why you find this piece of electronic equipment useful**

Or you may be given a very wide choice; a technological item being one of a number of appropriate alternatives:

> **Describe a thing you cannot live without.**
> **You should say:**
> **what it is**
> **how long you have had it**
> **what you use for**
> **and explain why you think you cannot live without this thing**

Describe something you use for your work or your studies.
You should say:
what it is
how you use it
how often you use it
and say if you would be able to do your work or studies without this thing

Useful domestic appliances

You need to be careful when distinguishing between technological items, electrical and electronic items, and household appliances. The people who set the part two questions will never try to trick you into making a mistake and it is usually obvious what type of object you will be expected to talk about. However, I have known students who are so eager to talk about technology that they have misinterpreted the cue cards.

The main thing to remember is that if a useful household object or domestic appliance is specified then it is not appropriate to interpret that as meaning a computer, smartphone, or television.

Here is such an example:

Describe the most useful household appliance that you have.
You should say:
what it is
how it works
how life would be without it
and explain why it is so important to you

Strategy

Household or domestic appliances include such things as dishwashers, washing machines, freezers, refrigerators, microwave ovens, and vacuum cleaners. These are not very interesting things to talk about and you can usually describe what these things do in less than thirty seconds. What you need to do is concentrate on the last two prompts. You will invariably be asked how such an object has an impact on either your life or the lives of other people, or possibly both, and here is your opportunity to tell a story.

There is one prompt in the above card, *how it works*, that I am not able to answer. It doesn't happen often but, if it does, just be honest and move on. The important thing is to acknowledge that you have read the prompt and are not merely ignoring it.

One-minute notes

- out of all of the white goods that we own, the one we find most beneficial
- having received a bonus ... we decided to
- splash out
- never do we buy
- make all our meals from scratch
- if you needed to be frugal ... then I would definitely ...

Sample answer

I suppose that out of all of the white goods that we own, the one we find most beneficial is our freezer. It's basically just a big white box which sits in the corner of the kitchen and, as I'm sure you know, it keeps food below zero degrees. This enables fresh food to be kept for long periods, almost indefinitely in some cases. As for how it actually works, to be absolutely honest I haven't got a clue. I just know it keeps everything very cold.

We used to have, and still do for that matter, a small freezer compartment at the top of the fridge but it was good for nothing more than making ice cubes. We have always wanted a proper standalone freezer and having received a bonus at work last year we decided to splash out on one. And I am absolutely delighted that we have because it's been money well spent. I'm not exaggerating when I say that it has revolutionised the way we buy and cook food.

Both of us enjoy cooking and we make all our meals from scratch. Never do we buy pre-prepared or convenience foods. The only problem with this is that it can be quite time-consuming. Both of us work and study and we are often not really in the mood to make a meal when we get home in the evening. So what we have done is to master the art of batch cooking. At the weekend, when we both have a day off, we cook big pots of things like curries, chillies, and pasta sauces. When we get going it's like a production line and we end up with all our meals for the following week in individual plastic containers. These go into the freezer. Effectively we do now have convenience meals on weekdays but with the advantage of knowing that they are made from fresh and healthy ingredients.

And there is one other reason the freezer is important to us, and that's money. Our local supermarket discounts items which are nearing their sell-by dates. We buy these in bulk and freeze them. If you needed to be frugal then I would definitely recommend buying a freezer.

Points to note

- *out of all of the white goods that we own, the one we find most beneficial ...*
This is a paraphrase of *useful household appliance that you have.*

White goods are large domestic appliances such as cookers and refrigerators. They are usually, but don't have to be, white.

- *sits in*

Sits in is an alternative way of saying *is located in* or *is found in*.

- *I haven't got a clue*

This idiom is often used by native speakers and it simply means that you have no knowledge of something. It's an alternative way of saying, *I don't know.*

- *good for nothing*

If something is *good for nothing* then it has no use. Alternatively, as in the sample, you may say that something is *good for nothing* apart from one aspect, the implication being that it is almost useless.

- *standalone*

A device capable of operating independently of another device.

- *having received a bonus at work last year we decided to ...*

The narrative sequence of the perfect participle followed by past simple.

- *splash out*

To *splash out* is a phrasal verb to describe spending money lavishly or extravagantly.

- *money well spent*

This is an idiom meaning that the expenditure was wise. You can also have *time well spent*. For example, *going to English classes was time well spent.*

- *never do we buy*

A negative adverbial construction.

- *make all our meals from scratch*

To *make from scratch*, as we have seen before, is to make something from the start with basic ingredients.

- *master the art*

The phrase *master the art of* something is to learn how to do something extremely well.

- *batch cooking*

This is preparing multiple portions of several meals at the same time and storing them for future consumption

• *buy in bulk*
If you *buy in bulk* then you buy large quantities of something, typically at a discount.

• *if you needed to be frugal ... then I would definitely ...*
A second conditional.
There are, incidentally, many adjectives in the English language to describe people who are careful with money. *Frugal* and *thrifty* have positive connotations whereas *parsimonious*, *stingy* and *miserly* are entirely negative

Similar cue cards

Here are some variations which don't specifically mention appliances but where you could use the same or similar material.

> Describe an invention that you think is useful to people.
> You should say:
> what the invention is
> who invented it and why
> how it is useful to people
> and say whether it is useful to you personally

> Talk about a piece of equipment or tool that you use mostly at home.
> You should say:
> what it is
> how you use it
> why it is important to you
> and explain how the equipment works

Clothes

Cue cards in this category will invariably ask you to either describe a special item of clothing that you have bought or the type of clothes that you like to wear on a regular basis. Here's an example of the former:

> Describe an item of expensive clothing which you have bought recently.
> You should say:
> what type of clothing you bought
> how much it cost you
> why you bought it
> and explain how you felt after you bought it

Strategy

This is an example of a cue card which I personally would not like to be given because the subject matter does not interest me. I also can't readily bring to mind an occasion when I bought an expensive outfit. What I would advise doing in such circumstances is to be creative and make up a story. In my sample, I have used a number of the idioms, collocations and phrasal verbs a native speaker would use, and I have also deliberately exaggerated some aspects of the story for comic effect. If you are confident enough to do it, and your English is good enough, there is no reason why you shouldn't try to amuse your examiner.

One-minute notes

- purchasing high-priced outfits
- seldom do I …
- there would have been dire consequences if I hadn't …
- smarten up
- after I had received the invitation I …
- bite the bullet

Sample answer

I should probably start by saying that clothes don't interest or excite me at all and I derive no pleasure from purchasing high-priced outfits. Because I'm a student I don't have to purchase smart clothes for work and seldom do I frequent the sort of places like fancy restaurants where there is a dress code. As a result, I tend to wear the same basic outfit all the time. This invariably means jeans, t-shirt, trainers and a hoody. When something wears out or needs replacing I go and get something that looks remarkably similar. My mother complains that I look scruffy, but I would prefer to say that I have a casual, if slightly dishevelled, appearance.

But last year my sister got married and there would have been dire consequences if I hadn't smartened up for the occasion. Spoiling her big day by turning up to the church in jogging bottoms wasn't an option.

And so after I had received the invitation I bit the bullet and marched into the most expensive and exclusive gentlemen's outfitters in town. To be honest I felt like a fish out of water and I was glad when the ordeal was over. But I ended up buying a very elegant navy-blue suit and I have to say that I felt quite pleased with myself even though I had to stump up over £400.

My mother was over the moon when she saw me in it and I did receive lots of compliments on my appearance. I think they were surprised to see me looking presentable for a change.

I must admit that I blanched at paying so much at the time, but it was worth it in the end. And to soften the blow I like to think of the expenditure as an investment. I've got some job interviews coming up so buying an expensive suit might just pay dividends.

Points to note

• *derive no pleasure*
Saying that you *derive no pleasure* from something is a less common and, I think, more elegant, way of saying that you don't like or enjoy it. You can also use the positive, for example, *I derive enormous pleasure from long walks in the country.*

• *purchasing high-priced outfits*
A paraphrase of *expensive clothing which you have bought.*

• *seldom do I …*
A negative adverbial.

• dress code
A *dress code* is a set of rules specifying what you should wear in specific circumstances.

• *wear out*
If something *wears out*, it has been used so much that it is no longer able to be used.

• *dishevelled*
This is a word meaning an untidy appearance. It doesn't have quite the negative connotations of *scruffy.*

• *there would have been dire consequences if I hadn't …*
A third conditional.
Dire consequences is a phrase and collocation meaning *terrible repercussions.*

• *smarten up*
Smarten up is a phrasal verb meaning to make yourself look neater and tidier.

• *after I had received the invitation I …*
A narrative sequence of past perfect followed by past simple.

• *bite the bullet*
To bite the bullet is an idiom meaning to endure an unavoidable unpleasant situation.

• *fish out of water*
An idiom for a person in a place or situation they are not used to or feel uncomfortable in.

• *end up*
To *end up* doing something is a phrasal verb that means that you do something that you did not intend or want to do.

• *stump up*
This is an informal phrasal verb with a very similar meaning to *fork out*. In both instances, you are paying for something reluctantly.

• *over the moon*
The idiom *over the moon* is used to describe a person who is extremely happy about something

• *blanch at*
If you *blanch at* something you hesitate before doing something you find unpleasant.

• *soften the blow*
If something *softens the blow* it makes an unpleasant situation less serious.

• *pay dividends*
This is an idiom meaning that something brings benefits at a later date.

Similar cue cards

> Describe an item of clothing that you like to wear.
> You should say:
> what it is
> what it looks like
> where you got it from
> and explain why you like to wear it

> Describe an item of clothing or jewellery that you wear on special occasions.
> You should say:
> what it looks like
> where you bought it
> on what special occasions you wear it
> and explain why you wear it on special occasions

Things produced in your country

If you can't think of something that is produced in your country then do some research now!

It doesn't have to be a manufactured product like a car, think also of agricultural products and foodstuffs that grow well in your region. Essentially it could be anything from tractors to olive oil but, if at all possible, try to think of something that is either unique to your country or something that it specialises in.

> Describe something that is produced in your country.
> You should say:
> what the product is
> what it is used for
> how it is made
> and explain why your country produces this thing

Strategy

It may be difficult to find a personal angle to these prompts and it is entirely possible that neither you nor members of your immediate family are involved in the production of something from your country. You could, therefore, choose to answer the points in order but one of my Portuguese students was a little more creative in the following response.

One-minute notes

- harvesting the commodity
- build up
- only then can you
- after they had selected a tree would
- from what I can gather …
- if nothing had been done it would now be in serious trouble

Sample answer

My grandfather had an unusual job when he was a young man and I'm still fascinated by the stories he tells of his time in the south of the country harvesting the commodity cork. Cork, essentially, is the bark of a particular variety of oak tree. These grow primarily in the south of the country and it has been a major industry in the area for centuries. It still is, and I think I'm right in saying that Portugal is the largest producer of cork in the world. The reason is because this type of tree grows well in our climate and soil and over the years we have built up the knowledge and skills to harvest it.

It's a totally sustainable industry because you don't have to chop down a tree to harvest the bark. First, you have to wait until the oak tree reaches a certain age and that's quite a long time. Only then can you safely remove the bark without causing damage. At that stage, you can take a section away and eventually it will grow back. I remember Granddad explaining that it was every ten years or so. What men like him did was to walk deep into the forest and after they had selected a tree would use sharp axes to slice off the outer covering from the trunk in a circle around it. So when they had finished it looked like the tree had a sort of collar.

From what I can gather it's quite a skilled job and if you don't know what you are doing then you can cause permanent damage to the tree. According to him, it's also back-breaking work because after the bark had been cut he then manhandled it out of the forest. You can't drive tractors into dense woodland.

What is it used for? Well, historically the cork was made into the little plugs that seal the tops of bottles of wine. Nowadays many wine producers use metal screw caps and for a while, the cork industry went into decline. If nothing had been done it would now be in serious trouble but fortunately, it's bounced back because new uses have been created for the material. Cork is quite attractive and waterproof and can be made into decorative wall tiles or even handbags.

Points to note

• *harvesting the commodity*
A paraphrase of *something that is produced*.

• *I think I'm right in saying that ....*
If you are not sure about a fact a useful phrase is, *I think I'm right in saying that ....*

• *build up*
To *build up* is a phrasal verb meaning, among other things, to develop something. It's separable so you could say, *they have built the knowledge up*.

• *only then can you*
A negative adverbial phrase.

• take away
This phrasal verb means to remove something from where it is. It's separable so an alternative in the sample above would be to say, *take away a section*.

• *grow back*
A phrasal verb meaning to begin growing again after being cut off or damaged.

- *after they had selected a tree would ...*

The narrative tense sequence of past perfect plus past simple.

- *slice off*

This is another separable phrasal verb and it means to remove a piece of something from the rest using a sharp object like a knife.

- *from what I can gather ...*

This is another phrase to use when you are presenting information you are not totally sure about.

- *back-breaking work*

This is work that is physically very strenuous and demanding.

- manhandle

The verb to *manhandle* is to move or lift a heavy object by hand using a lot of effort.

- *if nothing had been done it would now be in serious trouble*

This is a mixed conditional indicating present result of a past condition.

Similar cue cards

> Describe an important export item from your country.
> You should say:
> what it is
> how it is produced or manufactured
> what it is used for
> and explain why it is an important export item in your country

> Describe an industry in your country.
> You should say:
> what this industry is
> what is produced or manufactured
> where the industry is located
> and explain why it is an important industry in your country

Intangibles

Intangibles include such things as films, books, music, and TV programmes. The cue cards invariably take the form of, *Describe your favourite ....*

Incidentally, a book is, of course, tangible in one sense. It has a cover and pages and you can pick it up. However, if you are asked to talk about your favourite book the examiner will obviously expect you to describe what the book is about.

Here's a typical book example:

> **Describe a book you have recently read.**
> **You should say:**
> **what kind of book it is**
> **what it is about**
> **what sort of people would enjoy it**
> **and explain why you like it**

Strategy

If you are not asked about your favourite book, film or music in part two, then it is likely that you will be elsewhere in the test. It's, therefore, time well spent to think about these things in advance. You don't have to impress the examiner by choosing a scholarly literary work, an obscure art-house film or classical music. Stick to what you know and like.

One-minute notes

- it was last year on holiday when I was relaxing on the beach
- got around to
- get my teeth into it.
- only after a variety of ... does he ...
- types of people who would appreciate ...
- If you haven't already read it I would ...

Sample answer

It was last year on holiday when I was relaxing on the beach that I finally got around to reading David Copperfield by Charles Dickens. I've wanted to read it for years but was a little put off by the sheer size of the book. A fortnight's holiday seemed like a good opportunity to get my teeth into it.

David Copperfield is a novel considered to be one of the great classics of English literature. It's written in the first person and is essentially the story of a young man's life. I understand that it is autobiographical and loosely based on Dickens' own experiences, particularly the miserable events of his childhood. David, the hero of the story, is a relatively happy child at the beginning of the novel living in the countryside with his widowed mother. But after her remarriage, his life takes a turn for the worse.

His stepfather, his principal antagonist in the early part of the story, is responsible for sending David to a dreadful boarding school ruled over by a cruel headmaster. He's later sent to work in a factory in London where he has to endure harsh conditions. Only after a variety of extraordinary adventures over a number of years does he finally find the love of his life and success as a novelist.

As for the types of people who would appreciate this novel, well what perhaps is interesting is that it was originally written for ordinary working people whereas now it's considered to be a scholarly work of literature and is used primarily as a set book in schools. I think that's unfortunate because I'm sure it's a novel that can be enjoyed by people of any age.

Many of the themes are as relevant today as they were when it was written in the nineteenth century. It has comedy and tragedy in equal measure and the huge cast of characters is gloriously vivid. If you haven't already read it I would definitely recommend that you do.

Points to note

- *it was last year on holiday when I was relaxing on the beach*

As I have noted before, you don't always have to start with a paraphrase. There are often opportunities at the beginning of your response to start with the narrative tense sequence of the past continuous followed but the past simple. Here I am being asked to talk about a book I have recently read so I have chosen to say what I was doing at the time - *it was last year when I was relaxing that I ...*

- *put off*

To *put off* is a phrasal verb that means to delay doing something until a later time.

- *get around to*

This is a phrasal verb and it means to finally do something that you have been intending to do for some time.
You can often use this in conjunction with *put off*. For example, *I've been putting off decorating the kitchen for months, but I finally got around to it last week.*

- *get my teeth into*

The idiom *get my teeth into* something means that I am getting involved in something interesting or complex with great enthusiasm.

- *take a turn for the worse*

This is an idiom used to signify, unsurprisingly, that something got worse quickly.

- *only after a variety of ... does he ...*
A negative adverbial structure.

- *types of people who would appreciate ...*
Instead of paraphrasing the first line of the cue card, I have chosen the fifth, *what sort of people would enjoy it*.

- *in equal measure*
In equal measure can be used when the amount of one thing is the same as the amount of another thing. For example, *my high school headmaster commanded fear and respect in equal measure.*

- *if you haven't already read it I would ...*
A second conditional ending.

Here are some additional *things* cue cards.

> Describe a foreign film that you enjoyed watching.
> You should say:
> what type of film it was
> who the actors were
> what the film was about
> and explain what you like about this film

> Describe a TV program that you like to watch.
> You should say:
> what type of program it is
> when and how often you watch it
> what the contents of the program are
> and explain why you like this program.

> Describe a song that has special meaning for you.
> You should say:
> what song it is
> when you first heard it
> what the song is about
> and explain why this song has special meaning for you.

And finally

As always, please check the tense of the verb in the first line of the prompt. You may be asked about a thing you would like to have in the future. If so, I would recommend that you choose a thing that you have now, and therefore know about, and make the same adjustments that I describe for hypothetical journeys at the end of the places chapter.

Here's a sample cue card:

> Describe something special you want to buy in the future.
> You should say:
> what it is
> why it is special
> when you intend to buy it
> and explain why you want to buy it

And here's my response based on what I had prepared for my technology question.

I'm saving up for a smartwatch. I've wanted one since I saw my brother's a few months ago. As soon as he bought it he came to show me what it does. He's always been fanatical about the latest technology and adores gadgets, so it was inevitable, I suppose, that he would get one.

I was initially a little dubious and thought that smartwatches were nothing more than expensive toys for adults and I even read somewhere that they provide a solution to non-existent problems. I mean, why pay a lot of money for a smartwatch when it doesn't appear to do very much more than a smartphone? Okay, you can use a smartwatch to note the time, look at appointments in the calendar, check off boxes in a to-do list and read incoming text messages. But you can do all of those things on your phone.

And there are, of course, drawbacks. The screen on the watch is too small for anything but basic information so if you need to look up something on the internet or read the latest news then you need to look at your smartphone. I didn't use to understand why anyone would want to fork out a few hundred pounds for a clever watch.

But I have changed my mind and the reason is because of what I consider to be the watch's killer app. It has a heart rate sensor linked to an application which monitors what the beat is throughout the day. And because the watch also has a motion sensor it knows whether you are sitting, walking briskly or doing a heavy workout. It's sometimes important to know how quickly your heart rate returns to normal after you have been exercising and I would love to be able to do that when I'm at the gym.

There's a history of heart problems in my family so I would like to keep tabs on these things. This smartwatch, so my brother tells me, will alert you if it detects any abnormalities and potentially that could have lifesaving consequences. For me, that's an important enough reason for buying one and I should have enough money in a couple of months.

Experiences and Events

I have saved the most wide-ranging category for last. As such, it is difficult to subdivide, and you need to be prepared for outliers, those cue cards which refuse to fit neatly into a particular grouping. However, the majority of the speaking subjects under the broad heading of experiences, activities, and events fall into one of the following headings:

- **Personal experiences**
These are either specific incidents, such as *a time you went to a new school*, or you get to choose the actual experience subject to a certain parameter, for instance, *a time when you were very busy*.

- **Personal activities**
These are things that you do now or used to in the past. For example, *an activity that you do to stay healthy* or *a game you enjoyed when you were a child*.

- **Public events**
These include such things as festivals and sporting occasions

- **Historical events**

Specific personal experiences

Here is a typical example of a cue card where you are asked about a particular personal experience. Being asked questions about your own school days or the education of young people, in general, is common in all three parts of the speaking exam.

> Describe a time when you moved to a new school or home
> You should say:
> when you moved
> where you moved from and to
> why you moved
> and explain how you felt about this move

Strategy

This is an example of a cue card where there is potentially a huge imbalance between what you are able to say for one of the prompts in comparison to what you can say for the others. I can answer the first three in one sentence, *I moved from junior school to high school at the age of eleven because I had to.* There is no conceivable way that I can give equal weight to all four prompts. Don't worry if this happens. Just make sure that each point is covered, no matter how briefly, and expand on the one prompt which gives you the most scope for impressing the examiner. Quite clearly on this card, it is the final one.

One-minute notes

- transferring from junior to high school is …
- rite of passage
- grow into
- as I walked, I felt that people were laughing
- would have turned and legged it had …
- not only was I leaving behind

Sample answer

Transferring from junior to high school is one of those rites of passage that all of us have to endure when we are young, and it can often be somewhat traumatic. Well, it was for me. In the town where I grew up, all kids had to move to a new school at the age of eleven. I remember the day with remarkable clarity even though it was a long time ago. I was wearing a new uniform which wasn't at all comfortable because the blazer and trousers were several sizes too big. My mother said that I would soon grow into them.

It was a fair trek from my home. It took about twenty minutes, and as I walked, I felt that people were laughing at the sight of me in my obviously brand-new and ill-fitting outfit. Looking back, they probably weren't but you can be terribly self-conscious when you are a child.

When I set off from home I actually felt okay. There was even a bit of a spring in my step but gradually, the closer I got to the school, the confidence started to wane. By the time the building came into sight, I was having a serious case of cold feet. I would have turned and legged it had it not been for the fact that I would have been in serious trouble when my father found out.

I think there were a couple of reasons why I felt so anxious. Not only was I leaving behind a familiar and cosy little junior school where I had been blissfully happy, but my big new high school had a formidable reputation for academic excellence. I really did worry that I wouldn't be able to keep up. With the benefit of hindsight, I now realise that I had absolutely nothing to bother about. But change can be a difficult and scary thing, especially when you are a child.

Points to note

- *Transferring from junior to high school*
A paraphrase of *moved to a new school*

- *rite of passage*
An idiom signifying an important event in your life as you pass from one stage to another.

- *grow into*
A phrasal verb we use to describe what happens when we deliberately buy clothes for children which are a few sizes too large. Eventually, the child will grow into them.

- *a fair trek*
Using *fair* as an adjective meaning considerable in size but not huge is an example of precision vocabulary. If you say that you had a *fair trek* to school, then the walk was longer than you might expect but not totally unreasonable in the circumstances. It's a lot more precise than saying that you had a long trek to school.

- *as I walked, I felt that people were laughing*
The narrative tense sequence of past simple plus past continuous.

- *look back*
The phrasal verb *to look back*, meaning to think about an event in the past, can be used in many part two talks.

- *to walk with a spring in your step*
An idiom meaning that you walk energetically showing that you feel confident and happy.

- *to have cold feet*
An idiom meaning that you have lost your confidence.

- *I would have turned and legged it*
This is a third conditional structure which incorporates an informal phrasal verb. *To leg it* means to run away from something quickly, usually in order to escape.

- *Not only was I leaving behind ...*
A negative adverbial structure.

- *keep up*
The phrasal verb *to keep up* can have a number of meanings. Here it means to do as well as other people.

• *with the benefit of hindsight*
This is a phrase meaning having the ability to understand an event only after it has happened and not at the time.

Here are some more specific experiences cue cards:

> Describe a high school class or university course that you enjoyed.
> You should say:
> what the subject was
> where you studied it
> what the contents of the course or class were
> and explain why you enjoyed this subject

> Describe your first day at work or the place where you study
> You should say:
> what kind of building it was located in
> why it was important for you to work/study there
> how you felt at the end of the first day
> and explain if you were pleased or disappointed with the experience

> Describe a sports event that you took part in or watched
> You should say:
> what the event was
> where it was
> who was competing
> and explain how you felt about this event.

> Describe an occasion when visitors came to your home
> You should say:
> who they were
> why they visited your home
> how you spent the time with these visitors
> and explain how you felt about the visit.

Unspecified personal experiences

The themes on the cards in this category are wide-ranging but are usually about positive experiences, for instance, *describe a time when you were happy*. Occasionally, however, you may be asked about unfavourable circumstances. We will have a look at one of each starting with a typically positive example:

> **Describe a positive change in your life.**
> **You should say:**
> **what the change was**
> **when it happened**
> **describe details of the change**
> **and explain how it affected your life**

Strategy

With this card, you are given plenty of scope. Many students have chosen a new job or starting at university and both give you lots of opportunities for including interesting vocabulary and complex grammar. Note particularly that in cue cards which mention change you will essentially be talking about two experiences. You will need to describe what your life was like before the change and how it was different afterwards.

One-minute notes

- a hugely beneficial development
- stay put
- better the devil you know
- rarely do I
- it was only after I had … that I
- it would have been disrespectful if I had

Sample answer

Although I didn't realise it at the time, a hugely beneficial development in my life was moving to a new job last year. I used to work for a small company and I took satisfaction in what I did on a day-to-day basis. I had a great deal of autonomy and I got on well with my colleagues. Therefore, when I was headhunted by a much larger concern, making the decision to move or stay put was extremely difficult.

It didn't help that I was given conflicting advice by family and friends. My mother who is very risk-averse kept saying, 'Better the devil you know,' whereas my father emphasised the benefits of working for a considerably larger company. I was more inclined to his way of thinking but feared ending up as a cog in a machine.

Rarely do I make decisions quickly and it was only after I had given the matter a huge amount of thought that I eventually resolved to accept the new job. In the end, the deciding factor was that the new company had approached me. They had taken the time and trouble to find out about my skills and clearly believed that they were the perfect fit for the role they had available. In some respects, it would have been almost disrespectful if I had turned them down.

Only now do I realise that I made absolutely the right decision. I was reasonably happy in my old job, but I think I was just treading water most of the time. There were no opportunities for developing new skills and no real chance of promotion. In my new job, however, I have a well-defined professional development plan and career path. Change can be scary at times, but you can miss out on so many opportunities if you don't take the occasional risk.

Points to note

- *a hugely beneficial development*
A paraphrase of *a positive change*

- *headhunt*
The verb *to headhunt* has a very specific meaning in terms of jobs and employment. It means to identify and approach a person in a company and invite them to fill a position elsewhere.

- *stay put*
The phrasal verb *to stay put* means to remain in the same location or position.

- *risk averse*
A *risk-averse* person is somebody unwilling to take risks or wanting to avoid risks as much as possible.

- *better the devil you know*
This is an idiomatic phrase and it means that it is often better to deal with someone or something you are familiar with and know, even if they are not ideal than take a risk with an unknown person or thing.

- *cog in a machine*
The idiom, *a cog in a machine* is used to signify somebody who plays an insignificant role in a large organisation or operation.

- *rarely do I*
I have included two negative adverbial phrases, *rarely do I ...* and *only now do I ...*

- *it was only after I had ... that I ...*
The narrative tense structure of past perfect followed by past simple

- *turn somebody down*

The phrasal verb to turn somebody down means to decline to do what somebody asks or suggests.

- *find out*

To *find out* about something is a common phrasal verb meaning to get information about it.

- *it would have been almost disrespectful if I had ...*

A third conditional structure.

- *tread water*

An idiom meaning that you maintain your current status without making any significant progress.

- *miss out*

To *miss out* on something is a phrasal verb meaning to not get the chance to do something that you would have enjoyed or been beneficial to you in some way.

Cue cards with similar themes

> Describe a positive experience you had during your teenage years.
> You should say:
> what the experience was
> when it happened
> where it happened
> and explain why you think this was a positive experience

> Describe a recent event that made you feel happy.
> You should say:
> what the event was
> where it happened
> who was with you
> and explain why you think this event was so enjoyable

> Describe a situation when you helped someone.
> You should say:
> what the situation was
> who the person was
> how you helped them
> and explain how you felt after helping them

Describe a time when you were very busy
You should say:
when this time was
what you did at this time
how you arranged this time
and explain how you felt after this busy time was over

Let's look now at an example of an unfavourable personal experience cue card. These are quite rare but it's best to be prepared. Please note that I use the word *unfavourable* deliberately. You are not going to be asked about wholly negative experiences such as how you felt after a tragic event in your life.

Here's a typical example of a mildly unfavourable personal experience:

Describe a situation or time when you were late.
You should say:
what you were late for
why you were late
what you did about being late
and explain how you felt

Strategy

This is a cue card which clearly invites you to tell a story and the prompts steer you in the usual narrative sequence of a beginning, a middle and an end. There is no reason why, assuming you cover all the points, you should not add more information, so I will open my talk with how I usually feel about lateness in myself and others.

One-minute notes

- even the best-laid plans ...
- an occasion when I wasn't punctual
- looking back
- not until I arrived did I ...
- there had been ... which meant that
- if I had sat around ... normal service would have

Sample answer

I dislike unpunctuality in myself because I get very anxious if I am running late for something and I dislike it in other people because it's disrespectful. Keeping others waiting is ill-mannered and invariably avoidable with a little planning and good time management. Sometimes, however, even the best-laid plans go awry, and an occasion when I wasn't punctual was my brother's wedding day.

He got married on a Saturday afternoon last summer and it was in a city a two-hour train journey from my home. Looking back, I should have travelled on the previous evening and stayed in a hotel. But I looked up the timetables and saw that there were plenty of early-morning trains which would have got me to the wedding with hours to spare. I assumed everything would be fine. Not until I arrived at the station did I discover that my plans were about to go horribly wrong. There had been some sort of signalling failure which meant that the trains were not able to run. To make matters worse nobody in positions of authority in the place had any idea when the problem might be fixed.

It's possible that if I had sat around and waited normal service would have resumed but I really didn't want to take that risk. Unfortunately, I don't drive, otherwise I would have hired a car, so what I did instead was to run to the coach station. I hadn't prepared a plan B, but I did know that there were a couple of buses a day to where the wedding was to take place.

I managed to get a ticket for one, but it was a thoroughly unpleasant journey. It took a really circuitous route stopping in every village on the way. I was looking at my watch every few minutes and becoming more and more jittery as the hour of the wedding approached. In the event, I missed the service which was bitterly disappointing, but I did make it to the reception.

Points to note

• *even the best-laid plans go awry*
This is an idiomatic phrase which comes from a famous poem by the Scottish writer Robert Burns. It means that no matter how carefully you prepare for something, often things will go wrong.

• *an occasion when I wasn't punctual*
A good place for your paraphrase is at the beginning of your answer but it doesn't have to be. On this occasion, I have paraphrased the first line of the prompt, *a time when you were late*, a little later into my narrative.

• *looking back*
This, once again, is our useful phrasal verb meaning to remember something in the past.

• *with hours to spare*
A phrase used to indicate that there was plenty of time left over after an event or task.

• *not until I arrived did I …*
A negative adverbial structure.

• *there had been … which meant that …*
This is the narrative tense sequence of past perfect followed by past simple. First, the signals failed, then the trains stopped running.

• *to make matters worse …*
A phrase meaning that something made the existing difficult or unpleasant situation even more unfavourable.

• *sit around*
This is a phrasal verb and it has a more precise meaning than merely *sit* on its own. If you *sit around*, you spend time not doing anything useful.

•*if I had sat around … normal service would have …*
Here I have incorporated the phrasal verb into a third conditional sentence.

• *I don't drive, otherwise I would have …*
This is an example of a mixed conditional. It is a past result of a present and continuing condition. It is also a conditional where the if clause is implied. It is a shortened way of saying that, *if I were able to drive, I would have hired a car.*

• *plan B*
A synonym for an alternative strategy.

• *a circuitous route*
A synonym for a route or journey which is longer than the direct way.

• *jittery*
A good alternative for anxious and unable to relax.

• *make it*
This is an idiom meaning to arrive and is usually used in connection with time. For example, *we made it to the cinema just as the film was starting.*

Here's a similar unfavourable personal experiences cue card:

> **Describe something you once forgot to do**
> You should say:
> what you forgot to do
> when this happened
> where it happened
> and explain what you did about it

Personal activities

Cue cards in this category can vary greatly but often involve sports, hobbies, and skills. Fitness and health are common themes in all three parts of the test and here is a typical card:

> **Describe something healthy you enjoy doing**
> You should say:
> what you do
> where you do it
> who you do it with
> and explain why you think doing this is healthy

Strategy

There is a huge range of things which are supposed to be healthy. It doesn't have to mean regular sessions in the gym or the swimming pool. The first line of the card doesn't specifically mention activities, so *something healthy* could be interpreted as a diet full of fruit and vegetables or even meditation. I've chosen walking, however, because it gives me more opportunities to address the *where* and *who with* parts of the cue card.

One-minute notes

- The fitness activity I like the most
- after I'd heard about this, I decided …
- rope in
- not only is it good exercise but …
- if it wasn't for the app, we would all …
- fit as a fiddle

Sample answer

The fitness activity I like the most is walking. The government in my country always seems to be pushing some sort of health message and I usually take notice. Recently the big thing was 'five a day.' We were all encouraged to eat five portions of fruit or vegetables and I manage this quite easily. The latest message is that we should all walk ten thousand steps each day.

After I'd heard about this I decided to investigate because I didn't have a clue how many steps a day I did take. The great thing though is that it's quite easy to find out. Everyone has a smartphone these days and you can download a pedometer app. This is able to count your strides and tell you how many you have done and also what distance you have covered. I find it quite fascinating and, if anything, I've probably become a bit obsessive about it.

In the course of the day, I often do build up a fair number of steps but rarely ten thousand. Therefore in the evening, usually after dinner, I rope in the family members who are around to come with me on a walk. There's a park near our flat so we often go there. If it's raining, there's a covered shopping mall which stays open late. Not only is it good exercise but it's quite a sociable thing to do and we all seem to enjoy it. If it wasn't for the app, we would all spend the evening slumped in front of the television. If there's nobody around, then I go out on my own and I keep walking until I've reached the target.

I think that walking can easily be overlooked as a form of exercise. As long as you are moving along at a brisk pace there are huge health benefits. Apparently, regular walking can reduce the risk of heart disease and various cancers and also maintain normal blood pressure. I must admit that I am feeling as fit as a fiddle since I started.

Points to note

- *The fitness activity I like the most*
A paraphrase of something healthy you enjoy doing.

- *a big thing*
This is something that is important or prominent.

- *after I'd heard about this, I decided ...*
The narrative tense sequence of past perfect followed by past simple.

- *don't have a clue*
If you *don't have a clue* about something it means you don't know the answer.

- *find out*
This is a phrasal verb meaning to get information about something.

• *build up*
The phrasal verb *to build up* means to gradually increase in amount or size.

• *rope in*
This is quite an informal phrasal verb which shouldn't be used in IELTS writing. It's fine in speaking and means to persuade others to do something with you. It implies an element of unwillingness on their part.

• *Not only is it ...*
The ever-useful negative adverbial structure.

• if it wasn't for the app, we would all ...
A second conditional structure.

• *Fit as a fiddle*
An idiom meaning to be in extremely good health.

You are usually asked to talk about a personal activity you do in the present, as in the card above, but occasionally the focus is on the past as in this one:

> **Describe a useful skill you learned**
> **You should say:**
> **what it was**
> **who you learned it from**
> **how you learned it**
> **and explain why you think it is useful**

Strategy

Hopefully, you have noted, as with all cue cards, what tenses are used. Not only do you need to talk about learning the skill in the past, but you must also mention the implications of having this skill now in the present.

Examples of skills, meaning the ability to do something well, are numerous and I have heard students tackle this card in many different ways. Nowadays a lot of people interpret the word *skill* to mean something that you would include on a CV or resume, such as critical thinking or problem-solving. I would personally find it difficult to talk for two minutes about these types of what are sometimes referred to as soft skills. What is perhaps easier is to choose a practical skill such as being able to cook, make clothes or repair your car.

One-minute notes

- a knack for gardening which my father taught me
- turn your hand to
- inherited the house when a relative had died
- read up on
- not only do I ...
- given the chance, I would ...

Sample answer

I'm no expert but I do have a knack for gardening which my father taught me. He was an incredibly practical man and he could turn his hand to almost anything. With him, it was borne out of necessity because he didn't have a lot of money when he was bringing up a young family. We lived on what was almost a small farm and we kept livestock and grew vegetables. My father inherited the house when a distant relative had died and it was not in the best of condition. As you can imagine, there were always lots of things to be done and problems to be solved.

He was really successful at growing things and the vegetables always flourished. He definitely had green fingers and knew exactly what plants would grow in certain conditions such as in the shade or direct sunlight. He also read up on diseases and pests and how to control them safely and cheaply with such things as solutions of washing liquid. He was an organic gardener long before it became fashionable.

I used to spend hours with him in the vegetable garden because I found it fascinating and inevitably I learned a lot without deliberately intending to. Knowing how to grow and tend a kitchen garden is a skill which has stayed with me and when I moved house a few years ago I deliberately looked for one with a small plot of land. It's tiny in comparison to Dad's garden but I have a few rows of vegetables and a part set aside for herbs. It's absolutely great and I love it. Not only do I have really fresh organic produce, but I also save money on my supermarket bills. I also find it quite therapeutic spending a couple of hours pottering around amongst my plants after a day in the office. My only regret is that I don't have a little more space. Given the chance, I would definitely love to buy somewhere bigger.

Points to note

- *a knack for gardening which my father taught me*
A paraphrase of *a useful skill you learned.*

- *turn your hand to something*

This is an idiom. If you can *turn your hand* to a skill or activity, it means that you can do it well without necessarily having any experience.

- *borne out of necessity*

The verb to bear has two past participles which have different spellings. We use one, *born*, to refer to birth as in, *I was born in London*. The other, *borne*, is less common and is used in phrases such as *borne out of necessity*. This means that something happened or was established because it was in some way necessary.

- *inherited the house when a relative had died*

This is the narrative sequence of past simple and past perfect.

- *green fingers*

This is an idiom meaning you have a natural skill for growing plants.

- *read up on something*

This is a phrasal verb meaning to read about a particular subject because you want to know more about it.

- *Set aside*

A phrasal verb and it means something kept apart for a specific purpose.

- *not only do I ...*

A negative adverbial construction.

- *potter around*

This is a phrasal verb and it means to do small jobs in the house or garden in an unhurried and relaxed way.

- *given the chance, I would*

A conditional where the if clause is implied.

Similar personal activity cue cards

> Describe something useful you learned from a member of your family.
> You should say:
> what it was
> who you learned it from
> how you learned it
> and explain why you think it is useful.

Describe a sport you are interested in
You should say:
what people wear in this sport
what equipment is used
how this sport is played
and explain why you are interested in this sport

Describe an outdoor activity you would like to do for the first time.
You should say:
what the activity would be
where you would do it
what preparations and equipment you would need
and explain why you would like to do this activity.

Describe an interest or hobby that you particularly enjoy.
You should say:
what is it
how long have you been doing it
who you do it with
and explain why this is important to you.

Public events

These are typically festivals, celebrations, musical and sporting events which are celebrated by a large group of people in a particular city or locality or, indeed, by a whole nation. An example of a national celebration is asked for in the following common cue card:

Describe an important festival in your country
You should say:
when this festival is held
what people do during this festival
what you like or dislike about this festival
and explain why this is an important festival

Strategy

A large number of my students have chosen religious festivals when presented with this card. There is no reason why you shouldn't choose Christmas, Eid, Diwali or Hanukkah etc, but I would personally choose a celebration or commemoration which is unique to my country. As I have noted before, you won't get extra credit for entertaining your examiner, but it won't do any harm by attempting to engage his or her interest. I have, therefore, in the example below, chosen the uniquely British commemoration of Guy Fawkes Night.

One-minute notes

- one of our most significant and unusual national celebrations
- get rid of
- after having placed
- if he had .... Britain would have
- whale of a time
- rarely do the

Sample answer

One of our most significant and unusual national celebrations is Guy Fawkes Night, and, when I was a child, I absolutely loved it. It's peculiar to Britain and I'm fairly sure it's not celebrated anywhere else. It's held on the fifth of November, or sometimes on the nearest Saturday, and always in the evening. At that time of year, it gets dark quite early and it's invariably cold and so it's appropriate that the centrepiece is a huge bonfire. Preparations need to start some weeks beforehand because the materials for the fire have to be collected. I remember when I was young scrounging wood and pretty much anything combustible that neighbours wanted to get rid of.

On the evening itself, we would set light to the pile after having placed an effigy of a man called Guy Fawkes on top. The children invariably made these figures from old clothes stuffed with anything combustible so that they vaguely resembled a person. Guy Fawkes himself was a member of a gang who, over four hundred years ago, attempted to blow up the king and parliament in an event known as the Gunpowder Plot. If he had succeeded Britain would probably have a different official religion now.

Also, during the course of the evening, while we are warming ourselves by the flames, it is customary to eat anything that can be cooked easily in the fire such as baked potatoes. We also set off fireworks, which as a child I found especially thrilling. I had a whale of a time back then but nowadays I tend to get irritated by the noise. Rarely do the explosions finish before midnight. Having big fires and pyrotechnic displays in your back garden can also be quite hazardous and these days it is quite common to have carefully controlled public celebrations in local parks.

These days the event is possibly in decline, but I think it still has some significance as it has the potential to remind us of our turbulent history. If you are in Britain in early November, I would definitely recommend that you go to a Guy Fawkes celebration. It's a very unusual and highly entertaining part of our cultural history.

Points to note

• *One of our most significant and unusual national celebrations*
A paraphrase of *an important festival in your country.*

• *peculiar*
The adjective *peculiar* has two quite different meanings. It is most often used as a synonym for *odd* or *strange* as in, *if you don't keep milk in a fridge it can have a peculiar smell after a few days.* It can also mean something that is unique or particular and can be a very useful word when you are describing something that occurs only in your country or culture. Examples are, *Fado is a type of music peculiar to Portugal* and *Sashimi is a cuisine peculiar to Japan.*

• *scrounge*
A verb meaning to obtain something for no payment by simply asking for the item needed and relying on people's generosity.

• *get rid of*
This is a phrasal verb meaning to dispose of something.

• *after having placed*
A perfect participle used to convey a sequence of events.

• *blow up*
The phrasal verb *to blow up* means to destroy in an explosion.

• *If he had .... Britain would probably have*
This is an example of a mixed conditional denoting a present result of a past condition.

• *while we are warming ourselves ... it is customary to eat ...*
A narrative sequence of the present continuous followed by the present simple to describe a longer background action being interrupted by a new event.

• *set off*
A phrasal verb which can have a number of different definitions. Here the meaning is to make something explode.

- *having a whale of a time.*
An idiom meaning to enjoy yourself very much.

- *rarely do the explosions finish before midnight*
A negative adverbial construction.

- I have finished by using the conditional, *If you are in Britain in early November, I would definitely recommend...*

Cue cards with similar themes

> Describe an important traditional event in your culture or country.
> You should say:
> when this event is held
> who is involved in this event
> what people do during this event
> and explain why this event is important.

> Describe a musical event in your country.
> You should say
> what the event is
> where it takes place
> what kind of music is played
> and explain why you enjoy it.

Historical events

Cue cards inviting you to talk about a historical event are quite rare but, if you have the time, it would be useful to think about an event from the past that you would be able to describe. Even if this topic doesn't come up on a cue card, questions about history often arise in the final part of the exam.

Here is the usual way that the topic appears in part two.

> Describe an event in history that interests you.
> You should say:
> what happened
> when it happened
> how you know about this event
> and explain why it interests you.

Strategy

You have a great deal of choice about what to talk about. The historical period is not specified, nor is the location. As always, when you have limited time to prepare for part two, choose an event from your own country because this may be specified. The answer below is adapted from one given by a student from the Philippines.

One-minute notes

- significant incidents from the past ... quite fascinating
- not only were we visited but
- it was while he was working ...that he landed
- drum into
- If it had not been for ... it's unlikely that I would be ...
- a blessing in disguise.

Sample answer

I've always found significant incidents from the past which still resonate today quite fascinating and especially those in the history of my own country. Because of the strategic location of the Philippines, the country has always been at the centre of major trade routes. This has meant that since time immemorial the Philippines has been visited by travellers from all over the world. Not only were we visited but the country was also invaded and colonised a number of times.

It's one of these early visits that I would like to talk about and it is, for me, perhaps one of the most significant occasions in my country's history. This was the arrival of the Portuguese explorer Ferdinand Magellan. It was while he was working for the Spanish crown and attempting to find trading routes to the western Pacific that he landed in the Philippines in 1521. I know about this because it was drummed into us during history lessons at school and indeed any Filipino with only a vague interest in his or her country's history is likely to know of it.

Why it particularly interests me is because Magellan's arrival marked the beginning of Spanish interest in the Philippines. The country became a Spanish colony for over three hundred years and there are now many aspects of our day-to-day life, from cuisine to architecture to folk music, which have Hispanic influences.

From a personal point of view, perhaps the most significant long-term ramification of Spanish influence is our religion. If it had not been for Magellan it's unlikely that I would be Roman Catholic. This is the religion of the overwhelming majority of Filipinos and it's why many of our national holidays are also Catholic ones. I should also mention that the country was named in honour of the Spanish King Philip II. And last, but not least, my own surname has Spanish origins. This is perhaps the main reason why I am fascinated by my country's historical links with Spain which began with Magellan's arrival almost five hundred years ago. Regardless of his motives perhaps it was a blessing in disguise.

Points to note

- *I've always found significant incidents from the past ... quite fascinating*
A paraphrase of *an event in history that interests you.*

- *not only were we visited but ...*
A negative adverbial construction.

- *time immemorial*
A phrase meaning a time in the distant past beyond memory and record.

- *it was while he was working ...that he landed*
A narrative sequence of past continuous and past simple.

- *drum into*
A phrasal verb meaning to make somebody learn and remember something by repeating it often.

- *If it had not been for ... it's unlikely that I would be ...*
A mixed conditional signifying a present result of a past condition.

- *and last, but not least*
You can use this useful phrase to indicate that the last thing or person mentioned in the list is just as important as all the others.

- *a blessing in disguise*
Something that seems bad at first but has unforeseen positive outcomes.

Here are a couple of cue card variations. There is no reason why you can't use the same historical event but with minor modifications.

Describe a period in history which has always interested you.
You should say:
when it was
what happened in this period
why you are interested in it
and explain how you learned about it.

Describe an important event in your country's history.
You should say
when it happened
what the event was
who the most important people involved were
and what effect you think this event had.

PART THREE

Part three questions are considered to be more difficult than those in part one but, on the other hand, they do provide the best students with far more opportunities to display their English language skills.

This final part of the speaking test will last for approximately 4-5 minutes, roughly the same as part one. The format is also similar, so the examiner will ask you a number of questions to which you will be expected to respond, but there are a couple of key differences to note. The first difference is the subject matter and the second is the type of question you will be asked.

The subject that the examiner will ask you to talk about will be based on part two of the test. It's important to note that these questions in part three won't be based on your responses during part two, they are merely linked thematically to what was on the prompt card. So if, for example, the first line of the card had been, *Describe an old person that you know*, and you had spoken about your favourite grandfather, you will not be asked further questions about this particular person or, indeed, anything else that you had said. Instead, the examiner will use the theme of elderly people and ask questions about this subject.

These could, for example, be about how we look after elderly people in society or what role grandparents play in your particular country. You might also be asked about what age you think people should retire from full-time work or whether older people have any particular problems now that they didn't have in the past.

The questions are, therefore, potentially quite wide-ranging but they will all be linked to the same basic subject matter. The examiner won't suddenly switch from questions about old people to asking you about climate change.

As far as the type of questions is concerned, most are different from those in part one. In chapter nine we looked at how most of those part one questions are closed. In other words, they could be answered with a *yes* or *no* or a couple of words. The purpose of those questions is to seek information. Most questions in part three, on the other hand, are open questions and the purpose of most is to seek your opinions. You will still need to incorporate a range of more complex grammatical structures and less common vocabulary, but you will also need to consider the structure of your reply more carefully than you did at the start of the test.

I'm often asked about the ideal length for part three answers and whether you should aim for a certain number of sentences. Try, if you can, to aim for a bare minimum of three. Assuming your English is good enough this should always be possible because the questions in this part of the test are designed to assess your ability to expand your answers with explanations and examples. If you keep to the topic and remain fluent then don't worry too much about a maximum length. The examiner will control the timing and will move the conversation on.

The majority of the questions will fall into one of six categories which are detailed below. We will look at the strategies you should adopt and the types of phrases and structures you will need to use in order to achieve a high band score.

Categories of part three questions

1. Provide information

The first question that you may be asked might well be one which seeks further information on the general topic on the cue card. Although I noted above that most part three questions are open questions, it's possible that you might be given one which appears to be closed and similar to those in part one. The key thing here is to adopt a slightly different strategy. Instead of giving information and then qualifying it in some way as you would at the beginning of the test; ideally, in part three you should give also give an opinion. This will oblige you to use different phrases and structures.

Let me give you an example. If on the part two cue card you had been asked to talk about a work of art that you had seen, then your first part three question might be something like:

What kind of art do you enjoy?

Quite clearly the examiner is asking for information but in order to add a level of complexity to your answer, I would advise that you give an opinion. Here's a possible response.

Well, I enjoy looking at art from many periods from the Italian Renaissance through to the present day. However, as far as I'm concerned, contemporary art forces you to think more deeply. A landscape painting from say the eighteenth century might be aesthetically pleasing and technically accomplished but a modern-day abstract painting will challenge you. For me, it's far more intellectually stimulating which is why I especially like contemporary art.

And so although the question above is not very different from that which you might have been given in part one, the sample answer very definitely belongs to part three. The official IELTS website states that the final part gives you the opportunity *to talk about more abstract issues and ideas,* and your challenge is to take that opportunity even if the question also allows an 'easy' answer.

Here are a couple more examples of part three provide information question and sample answers:

Examiner:
What is a balanced diet?

Candidate:
This is also sometimes referred to as a healthy diet and it's said to be one which includes all the necessary vitamins and minerals and has things like protein and carbohydrate in the correct proportions. In all honesty, though, my impression is that there isn't a definitive answer. The science is contentious and even the so-called experts change their minds. I think there are too many variables at play and foods that might have some beneficial effects can also have detrimental ones.

Examiner:
What social problems are there in your country?

Candidate:
According to the media here, we are blighted by inequality, poor educational standards and a lack of employment opportunities. My own feeling on the subject is that these issues are not peculiar to my country. In an era of globalisation, free movement of capital and linked economies it's inevitable that social problems won't be confined to a particular country or region. It's absolutely true that there is a huge disparity in income between the wealthiest and the poorest people here, but this is a growing problem throughout the world.

We will look in more detail at the language you can use to express your opinion in the following section.

2. Giving your opinion

During part three of the test, I would encourage you to offer your opinions even though you might not be directly asked to do so. This is the tactic recommended above.

However, it is very common in part three to be directly asked what you think about a certain subject and there are two key things to remember when you are giving your responses. The first is to vary your language. There are many different alternatives to saying, *I think that.*, and I have listed a number of options at the end of the section.

Secondly, you need to extend your answers. You should say why you think in a certain way or have a particular belief and you should give examples where appropriate. In addition, you should be prepared to make concessions. In other words, you should acknowledge why there may be different opinions and give reasons why others might disagree with you.

Here are some four examples of part three opinion-type questions and sample answers which might follow on from the four main categories of part two topics - people, places, things, and experiences:

Examiner:
Does the younger generation lack respect for older people?

Candidate:
As far as I'm concerned, I'm convinced that the way younger people treat the elderly is very little different now from how it was in the dim and distant past. The notion that young people are disrespectful is not new. You only have to read social history books to realise that older adults have always thought that the younger generation is ill-disciplined, badly behaved and intolerant. It seems to me that there is also a tendency for older people to view their own past through rose-tinted specs. They like to imagine that they were always courteous and respectful to their elders when they were young but in reality, I suspect this was not always true.

Examiner:
Should people be charged to enter museums?

Candidate:
I can fully appreciate why many museums have to make an admission charge. They are, after all, expensive to run and somebody has to pay. If it is not the people who visit these institutions, then it invariably has to be the taxpayers. However, I have no doubt that it is in the interests of everyone that cultural and educational institutions such as museums and libraries should be free to all. Such places inspire learning, especially in the young, and help to broaden horizons. I firmly believe that access to knowledge should be free to all,

not just to those people who can afford it.

Examiner:
Do you think advertising has much influence over what people buy?

Candidate:
I like to think that I am totally immune to the power of advertising and that I am able to make up my own mind about the products and services that I purchase by carefully weighing up the pros and cons. However, I have the feeling that I might be fooling myself. Like most people, I develop irrational preferences for things which are familiar and I'm sure that adverts work on our unconscious mind by constantly exposing us to particular brand names and logos. It's therefore inevitable that when we are making purchasing decisions, we are inclined to select the names that we know. Above all, I'm sure that companies wouldn't spend millions on advertising unless it worked.

Examiner:
Do you think that your teenage years are the best years of your life?

Candidate:
I believe we should be wary about making sweeping generalisations like this one. It's undoubtedly true that some people have idyllic teenage years. After all, you are likely to be physically fit, free from responsibilities and not stuck in a boring job. On the other hand, you have very few freedoms. Most aspects of your life are beyond your control. You have no choice about whom you live with and some teenagers have a miserable time at school which they can do nothing about. You can't choose to up sticks and move to a different city. I think I'm going to sit on the fence on this one and say that it all depends. After all, your happiness at any age depends upon a multiplicity of factors.

Useful phrases to express your opinion:

As I mentioned at the start of this opinion section, try not to overuse the phrase, *I think that ...* There are lots of possible alternatives which include:

- *In my opinion, ...*
- *To my mind, ...*
- *As far as I am concerned, ...*
- *From my point of view, ...*

- *I would say that ...*
- *It seems to me that ...*
- *I am under the impression that ...*
- *I have the feeling that ...*
- *I have no doubt that ...*
- *I am certain that ...*
- *It goes without saying that ...*

3. Expressing causality

The causality type of question is essentially a specialised subset of the opinion type. These questions often begin with *Why ...?* and you are being asked why you believe something is the way that it is. You will need to explain what caused a particular situation or set of circumstances. You will probably use the word *because* but also try to adopt alternatives such as:

- *So*
- *Since*
- *As a result*
- *Due to*
- *Owing to*
- *Consequently*
- *As a consequence*
- *The effect of*
- *Therefore*

Please also note that there may be an opportunity to include a conditional phrase in your answer. I have done so in the sample answers from typical part three questions.

Examiner:
Can you suggest why some school children don't like going to school?

Candidate:
I believe that one of the main problems with junior schools, in particular, is that most are obliged to adopt a one size fits all strategy. Everything tends to be geared towards the average child. However, the school might have one child who is a mathematical genius but hates sport and another who has the potential to be a great footballer but can't understand simple multiplication. Potentially both kids could be unhappy because their specific needs aren't being met and this is a consequence of a lack of resources. If the school had more teachers and more money, they could identify individual learning

requirements and provide tailored solutions. Unfortunately, I can't see this happening anytime soon and as a consequence, you are always going to have unhappy students.

Examiner:
Why do so many people move from rural areas to live in large cities?

Candidate:
All four of my grandparents were born and grew up in small villages in rural areas and their forebears had lived there for generations. These ancestors worked on the land as farmers or in traditional agrarian trades such as blacksmiths. If such types of work had been available to people of my grandparent's generation, they might well have stayed where they were born. This didn't happen because there was a sea change in farming practices. Everything is mechanised, there are no horses and as a result, you need very few people to work the land. People have also broadened their horizons, probably as a result of films and television, and the bright light of the big cities has lured them away from what they might perceive to be a dull life in the countryside.

Examiner:
Why do you think some people are materialistic?

Candidate:
To be honest I think the modern-day obsession with material possessions is primarily a result of increasing standards of living in many countries. We have steadily moved from a hand-to-mouth existence to most of us having high disposable incomes. As a result, we have more money to buy things. It's probably as simple as that although you probably also have to factor in the power of advertising and peer pressure. If, for example, your friends have the latest phones and your neighbours buy a new car then you will probably want to keep up with them. We are becoming increasingly unable to know the difference between want and need.

Examiner:
Why do many people enjoy eating in restaurants?

Candidate:
I'm sure that there are a lot of reasons but one of the main ones is that people are far more interested in food than they used to be. As a consequence, they want to try cuisines from around the world, but they don't necessarily have the time or the inclination to cook such

meals at home. It's likely that they don't have the skills or knowledge to do this either. Another major reason is that cooking and eating at home for many people is just a routine event, almost a chore. However, if you eat in a restaurant other people will do the hard work. The ambience is usually conducive to a feeling of relaxation and the waiting staff, if they are good, will pamper you and make you feel special. And the cherry on the cake for me is that somebody else will do the washing up.

4. Talking about the past

In part three you may be asked to describe how things used to be in the past or, more likely, how things have changed during a certain period of time. To answer effectively you need to have a good command of the past tenses and, ideally, a knowledge of the structures, *used to + infinitive* and *would + infinitive*.

Here are four common part three questions with sample answers:

Examiner:
How has technology changed the way we work?

Candidate:
My mother's first job was as a clerical assistant in a big legal firm. I understand from the stories she has told about her time there that she was one of dozens of people, mainly women in that era, who used to spend their working days doing quite simple repetitive work such as copy-typing documents and then filing them away. There were whole armies of people in most companies and organisations who laboriously kept tabs on information and endlessly shuffled pieces of paper around. Technology has radically changed all that. Even the most senior people in pretty much any company, type their own letters and memos, they can send them to recipients instantaneously and keep copies in a shared drive. As a consequence, there is no need for people to perform clerical roles. This is mirrored in factories where robots can perform simple tasks that used to require manual labour.

Examiner:
How and why have holidays changed in the last fifty years?

Candidate:
Well, in my country people of my grandparent's generation did use to go on holiday but it was only for about one week each year and they didn't go very far, it was invariably to one

of the coastal resorts in their country a relatively short train journey from where they lived. There were two main reasons for this. First, they weren't given very much paid leave from their jobs and secondly, they didn't have a big disposable income. Consequently, their holiday options were very limited. I'm sure that if they had been richer, they would have been more adventurous but most people in those days weren't rich. Nowadays, however, people are far more affluent and the equivalent of one month's paid vacation is the norm. The result of this is that people can fly off to spend two weeks exploring exotic locations or just relaxing in the sun at a resort hotel, things unheard of half a century ago.

Examiner:

How is food shopping in your country different now from how it was in the past?

Candidate:

My grandparents have often spoken about their experiences of food shopping when they were younger. It sounds as though it was quite laborious and time-consuming. My grandmothers, in particular, used to visit a number of different small shops to buy such things as meat, fish, bread, and groceries and there was very little choice. Most of the produce was locally grown or produced and fresh fruit and vegetables had to be in season. Nowadays we are able to visit a large supermarket where we can buy a huge variety of foods from around the globe. It's made a huge difference to what we are able to cook and eat. My grandmothers would make a simple meal which was typical of the region using local ingredients. My generation, on the other hand, can buy the ingredients for recipes from all over the world.

Examiner:

What kinds of improvements have there been to transport in your country in recent years?

Candidate:

Well, congestion on the roads used to be a major problem, particularly in the larger cities, and this was a direct consequence of far more people being able to afford to buy and run private cars. Air pollution was also rising to unacceptable levels in urban areas. And so what the government did was to adopt a carrot-and-stick approach. First, to encourage the use of public transport, they invested heavily in new fleets of environmentally friendly buses. These are relatively cheap to use, and they are also reliable because they run on newly constructed bus-only lanes. There is also a new network of cycle tracks which makes travelling by bike in urban areas safe and quite pleasant. As for the stick, you now have to pay to bring a car to the centre of most cities and it's expensive. Most people opt for the cheaper option of catching the bus or cycling. All in all these improvements have made city centres far more pleasant places.

5. Talking about the future

Instead of talking about how things have changed in the past, you may also be asked to speculate on how they might change in the future. Try to avoid the easy option of saying, *I think X will happen.* There are lots of alternatives:

- *It's likely that …*
- *It's unlikely that …*
- *I imagine that …*
- *The chances are that …*
- *It is predicted that …*
- *My guess is that …*
- *It is possible that …*
- *It is probable that …*
- *I envisage that …*

In addition, these types of questions are an excellent opportunity to display your knowledge of conditionals. I have incorporated one into each of the four following sample answers to part three questions.

Examiner:
How do you think the family will change in the future?

Candidate:
It's likely that the changes to families we have already seen in my country as in others will continue. If affluent and well-educated young men and women are equally successful in climbing career ladders, then they are likely to have children at a later stage in their lives. And they will probably have fewer. The days of women staying at home to look after lots of children will come to an end and a couple having just one child in their thirties may well be the norm. In addition, I imagine that people will become increasingly mobile and eager to move to other cities and even countries for better opportunities and so having a big extended and supportive family living nearby will become an exception rather than the rule. I already know of many grandchildren who don't live in the same country as their grandparents and some don't even speak the same language.

Examiner:

Do you think there will be less sickness and disease in the future?

Candidate:

It's inevitable that research into vaccines and drugs will continue and hopefully, there will be big advances in medicine. If this happens then it's probable that cures will be found for many diseases which blight us now. The problem, however, is that medical science always seems to be playing catch up. It's wonderful that so many infectious diseases such as polio and smallpox have been pretty much been eradicated in most parts of the world but the result of this is that people live longer. This is obviously a good thing, but we are now having to deal with the illnesses of old age, such as dementia, which was not so much of a problem in the past. Overall my guess is that there may well be less sickness overall in the decades to come but that we may be plagued by diseases which are unknown to us now.

Examiner:

What do you imagine public transport will be like fifty years in the future?

Candidate:

To be honest I think that the answer to this question will vary enormously according to what part of the world we are talking about. In affluent economically developed countries, I envisage that local and state governments will invest heavily in environmentally friendly rapid transport systems such as trams, metros and light rail. The aim will be to ensure that travelling by public transport is cheaper, more convenient and faster than using a private car. If this happens then making journeys by mass transit systems will become the default for the majority of daily commutes to work and around urban areas for leisure. In poorer and less economically developed parts of the world, I fear that public transport will remain much the same as it is now.

Examiner:

What do you think might be the result in the future if most people buy everything online?

Candidate:

If the majority of people purchase all that they need online then potentially the biggest, and potentially most damaging outcome, will be the death of town and city centres as we know them today. It's likely that traditional bricks and mortar shops will close. We are already seeing the start of this process in many parts of the world and even many big out-of-town shopping malls have had to shut their doors. A regrettable consequence of this, I believe, will be the end of the traditional shopping streets and malls as social spaces. Currently, these are as much places to meet friends and relatives as they are places to buy things. Shopping online essentially means shopping in our own homes and a result of this is that people won't have to venture outside. This, I'm sure, will have negative effects on our physical and mental health.

6. Making comparisons

There are a couple of things that you need to be particularly aware of when answering questions where you are required to make a comparison between two things.

First, you must be sure that you know how to form comparative adjectives. If in any doubts please research and revise the grammar. Make sure you know which adjectives are irregular, which ones add *...er* in the comparative form and which are preceded by *more*. This is considered fairly basic grammar at A2 level and you simply can't afford to make any mistakes in IELTS.

Secondly, be aware of the linking expressions you can use to make comparisons. Try, as far as possible, to vary them in the same answer. Here are the most common ones:

- *On the other hand ...*
- *Whereas ...*
- *Nonetheless ...*
- *Having said that ....*
- *In contrast to ...*
- *Although ...*
- *In spite of ...*
- *However ...*

Here are some common questions and answers:

Examiner:
What are the differences between white-collar and blue-collar jobs?

Candidate:
Traditionally people, and men in particular, who wore white shirts in the workplace were in managerial or supervisory positions. They would invariably have been educated to degree level or, at the very least, have some qualifications. On the other hand, it was a custom for people doing manual labour to wear blue shirts. They were likely to have left school at the earliest opportunity with minimal paper qualifications. The key difference was whether you

worked using your brain or whether you used your hands. White-collar staff were to be found in offices and the blue-collar workers were in factories or warehouses. This rigid distinction is, I believe, dying out as the nature of work rapidly changes. In particular automation and the decline of heavy industry have massively reduced the need for manual labour, especially in developed economies.

Examiner:

When you are away on holiday what is the difference between staying with relatives or friends and staying in a hotel?

Candidate:

A major advantage of staying with friends is that you will minimise your holiday expenditure. This will appeal particularly to younger people and those travelling on a limited budget. Friends can also be an invaluable source of information and they will be able to point out such things as the best restaurants and the most interesting attractions to visit. On the other hand, not everyone likes staying in the houses of other people, even if they are close friends or relatives. There might be restrictions about when you can come and go and at what times you are able to eat. You have to take into account the timetables and routines of your host. However, if you stay in a hotel you are free to do pretty much what you want when you want. It's also likely to be more comfortable with such things as en-suite facilities and room service. Sleeping on a friend's couch might be cheap and cheerful but it tends to lose its appeal as you get older.

Examiner:

What are some of the differences between working for a big company and working for a smaller one?

Candidate:

If you are an employee of a large company, it's highly likely that it will have a clearly defined career structure in place. Therefore if you are diligent and ambitious you will probably be able to rise through the ranks. It's not unknown in some major businesses in my country for people to start off on the shop floor and end up sitting at the boardroom table. On the other hand, there are unlikely to be these opportunities in smaller organisations. If it's a family-run business, it may be impossible to achieve the highest levels of management because the son of the owner will always take precedence. However, one characteristic of the small concern, which is likely to be lacking in the larger one, is the much closer relationship that exists between the members of staff. This is in stark contrast to the big company where you might feel like you are just a minor cog in an uncaring machine.

Examiner:
What are the differences between big shopping malls and smaller local shops?

Candidate:
Shopping malls became popular because they are, in many respects, very convenient. If you have a car, they are usually easy to get to because they are situated away from congested urban areas and there is ample free parking. Driving to small local shops, on the other hand, can present problems. You might be faced with traffic hold-ups in the suburban streets and parking can be difficult to find. There might also be a charge. A mall also has a wide range of large shops under one roof, so you are likely to find everything you need without worrying about inclement weather whereas you will have less choice and might have to dodge the wind and rain if you shop locally. Having said that many people dislike shopping malls and I think it's primarily because the majority of the shops are branches of large chains. Shopping malls seem to be much of a muchness. Small local shops though tend to be family owned and each one is unique. You are likely to get a much higher level of personal service as there is a greater chance that the staff will get to know you.

APPENDIX ONE - FIFTY USEFUL PHRASAL VERBS

The questions in this appendix are all taken from IELTS part one. In addition to looking at how the phrasal verb has been incorporated into the answer please also take note of the use of the more unusual vocabulary and complex grammatical structures which will help you to high band scores in the test.

Bring up - to look after and educate a child

Examiner:
Do you often visit your hometown?

Candidate:
I very rarely do now because, although I was born and brought up in Cadiz in the south of Spain, my parents moved away to the north when they both retired. I visit them as often as I can which doesn't leave me with many opportunities to go back to Cadiz. I tend to go there only for the weddings of my cousins who are still there.

Ask around - to ask several people about something in order to find the help or information that you need.

Examiner:
Do you intend to change your job in the near future?

Candidate:
Well, to be honest, my current job is only a stopgap. It's not particularly well paid considering the long hours that I work and there aren't many opportunities for promotion or advancement. I've already started networking and making informal approaches to other employers. Often jobs aren't advertised, and you only find out about them by asking around.

Back up - to prove that something is true

Examiner:
Why is exercise good for you?

Candidate:
There's overwhelming medical evidence that backs up the proposition that exercise is

beneficial. But you don't really need the scientific evidence. I joined a gym last year and I started to feel the positive effects almost immediately. People tell me that I look better and I've certainly lost weight. Supposedly exercise lowers the risk of a number of diseases and I certainly feel healthier and more energetic.

Call off - to cancel an arranged event from taking place, usually because of a problem.

Examiner:
Do you prefer rainy days or sunny days?

Candidate:
This is an easy question for me to answer. I absolutely love the sun and adore outdoor activities such as going for walks in the country or taking a picnic to the beach. You can't really enjoy either of those if it's raining. I also play tennis a lot in the summer and take part in amateur tournaments. The big problem though is the unpredictability of the weather in this country. Quite often we have to call off matches at short notice because of the rain.

Carry on - to continue doing something.

Examiner:
How long have you been studying English?

Candidate:
I first started learning English at high school when I was about eleven. It was part of the curriculum, so I didn't have much choice. There was then a gap when I was at university because I simply didn't have time for anything other than my degree course. I started my language studies again recently because I need English for my job and I intend to carry on learning until I'm at least at C1 level.

Carry out - to do something that you have planned, especially something that you have said you will do or been told to do.

Examiner:
Are you good at practical tasks like DIY?

Candidate:
I really wish that I was because I would save so much money. Unfortunately whenever I try to carry out a simple repair job in the house something inevitably goes wrong and I flood

the place, or all the lights go out. It's invariably better if I call a professional.

Catch on - to become popular or fashionable.

Examiner:
Are bicycles popular in your country?

Candidate:
Oh, definitely and particularly in the last decade or so. When I was young people only tended to use bikes for short journeys as an alternative to using the bus or because they count afford a car. And you didn't see many adults on bikes often - it was mainly kids going to school. Nowadays cycling as a purely recreational activity has caught on in a big way. You see whole families going off on bikes into the countryside. I think it's part of the general trend for people to do healthy activities in their leisure time.

Catch up - to get the latest information about a subject

Examiner:
What are the benefits for you of using a computer?

Candidate:
There are a huge number of benefits to me personally. For one thing, it's great for making boring and routine tasks easier. I use spreadsheets, for example, to keep track of my finances and my spending. I've also got a database with all the contact details of my relatives and friends. Above all, I suppose it's the internet that has made the biggest difference. It's so much easier to buy things online than having to go to the shops. I also don't have to buy a newspaper anymore because I can catch up with all the news on my laptop.

Check up on - to try to find out if a person is doing what they should be doing

Examiner:
Do you think there should be restrictions on the use of the internet by children?

Candidate:
The internet can be a great resource for children and it can help them with their homework or just finding out about things that interest them. But there is also so much material that's totally inappropriate for young people to be looking at. You also hear about

things like cyberbullying and predators in chat rooms. So I definitely do think that you need to restrict what children are doing online but it's actually quite difficult. I don't like to keep checking up on my kids every ten minutes and so I've installed special software which stops them from accessing certain sites.

Come across - to find a thing or meet a person by chance and unexpectedly.

Examiner:
What historical event do you find most interesting?

Candidate:
I tend not to watch a lot of television, but I recently came across a fascinating documentary on the English Civil War. I had no idea how much it affected the lives of virtually everyone in the country. And it wasn't a straightforward division between, for example, the ruling class and the poor. Many families had divided loyalties with sons fighting on opposite sides.

Come up with - to think of an idea or plan or solution

Examiner:
In your work do you think you are more productive in the morning or the afternoon?

Candidate:
I have always been a morning person, even as a teenager which I know is unusual. Fortunately, we are allowed a certain amount of flexibility at my work we can pretty much start and finish when it suits us as long as we get the work done. And so I get there early in the morning. My brain seems to function far better then, and I find it a lot easier to come up with ideas and solutions to problems.

Count on - when you find a person totally reliable and able to help you in most situations.

Examiner:
How well do you know your neighbours?

Candidate:
We don't have too many neighbours because we live in a relatively small apartment block. But the ones we do have are great and some have become good friends. This can be

extremely convenient at times because we know we can count on them to look after our cat and water our plants if we need to go away for a few days. And, of course, we do the same for them.

Cut down on - to reduce the consumption of certain foods or drinks, often for health reasons.

Examiner:
What is your favourite food?

Candidate:
I have always enjoyed a good tender beef steak cooked rare and preferably served with chips and mushrooms. I know it's not particularly healthy and we as a family are cutting down on red meat. But it's still my meal of choice on special occasions.

Deal with - to take action in order to solve a problem or to ensure that something is done correctly.

Examiner:
What do you have to do in your job?

Candidate:
Primarily I have to deal with customer enquiries and occasionally complaints. Many people don't understand their monthly bills, so I try to explain what amounts we will take from their bank accounts and when. Also, some customers want to either upgrade or downgrade their service and I make the necessary amendments to the IT system.

Do away with - to discard something or stop doing or using something.

Examiner:
Do you think people today have a bigger workload than people did several decades ago?

Candidate:
I don't think that people necessarily have a larger workload than in the past, but the nature of the work has definitely changed. Technology and automation have done away with lots of manual and routine tasks but that doesn't mean we are doing less. I think we are having to use our brains far more.

Drop by - to visit a place, usually briefly and without a specific invitation.

Similar to **Drop in on** - to visit a person informally without the visit being pre-arranged.

> Examiner:
> *How much time do you spend with your family?*

> Candidate:
> *Family life is hugely important to me and so I like to spend as much time as possible with my parents and siblings. Things will inevitably change when I get married and have children but at the moment many of my evenings and weekends are free. After I've finished work, I often drop in on my parents on my way home and the whole family gets together on Sunday for a big lunch.*

End up - to arrive in a place without planning to, possibly because you have lost your way

> Examiner:
> *What kind of places do you like to travel to?*

> Candidate:
> *I'm not very keen on the sort of places that attract huge numbers of tourists and I dislike big cities. I much prefer smaller towns where the local people live and work. When I visit a country, I don't do much planning and often catch buses and trains to places I know very little about. I've ended up in some totally fascinating towns and villages and you get to appreciate the local culture far more that way.*

Factor in - to include a particular thing or amount when calculating something or making a judgement.

> Examiner:
> *Is the public transport in your city good?*

> Candidate:
> *It's good in the sense that it is efficient and reliable, and we have an excellent network of trams and bus routes. But you also need to factor in the cost. Recently there have been big increases in fares and that is obviously not so good. I would rather sacrifice the high frequencies on some routes in exchange for cheaper tickets.*

Find out - to get information about something, either by chance or by consulting books, the internet etc.

Examiner:
How do you feel about advertisements?

Candidate:
I found out recently that we each see something like 4,000 adverts a day. There has been a huge increase apparently because of digital marketing. Some people get really annoyed about this and find them intrusive, but I'm not too bothered. I actually tend not to notice them after a while.

Get across - to succeed in making a person understand a message or idea

Examiner:
How often do you eat fruits and vegetables?

Candidate:
Well, I certainly eat far more than I used to. The government has been getting across the message that we should all eat at least five a day because it has long-term beneficial effects on our health. I don't always manage that but there's never a day when I don't eat some fruit and vegetables.

Get along with - to have a friendly relationship with a person.

Examiner:
Do you do anything with your colleagues after work?

Candidate:
I get along with most of my colleagues really well and particularly the four in my immediate team. We've made a habit of going out immediately after work on a Friday. Sometimes it's a bar or we might go for a pizza. I really enjoy it and I think there are benefits from knowing your workmates socially.

Get around - to find a way of dealing with a problem by avoiding rather than actually solving it.

Examiner:
Do you prefer to study in a silent environment or in a place that has some noise?

Candidate:

Given the choice, I would much prefer to study in absolute silence because I am too easily distracted by noise. Unfortunately, this is rarely possible. At my university hall of residence, I can always hear music from neighbouring rooms which makes studying difficult. I can hardly go to every room and ask people to turn their music down, so I get around it by wearing earplugs.

Get away with - to escape blame or punishment or to avoid harm or criticism as a result of doing wrong.

Examiner:

Do you think it's good to take children to restaurants?

Candidate:

I'm sure the children usually enjoy it but unless it's a place like a fast food restaurant I don't think parents should take young kids out for meals. A couple of times now I've been in restaurants and children have been running around the place, making lots of noise and disturbing everyone. And the parents let them get away with it which I find very surprising and annoying.

Get back into - to become interested in something again

Examiner:

Do you play any particular sport?

Candidate:

When I was young, I used to play basketball, but I stopped when I went to university because I didn't have the time. But I've recently got back into it because I knew I needed the exercise.

Get by - to have or know enough to survive in a particular situation but not enough to make it easy.

Examiner:

Do you enjoy being a student?

Candidate:

I'm passionate about my subject and I can happily spend hours in the library, but the financial aspects worry me. I have a part-time job in a restaurant and just about get by but not having enough money is a constant source of anxiety.

Get rid of - to eliminate or discard

Examiner:

What would you like to change in your hometown?

Candidate:

I can't see it happening, but I would love to get rid of some of the ugly concrete office blocks that were built in the 1970s. They really spoil the look of the historic centre.

Get around to - to finally find time to do something you have been intending to do for some time.

Examiner:

Do you like drawing or painting?

Candidate:

I used to love art classes when I was at school, but I don't paint or draw now. I would love to if I had the time and it's something I intend to get around to when I have a lighter workload.

Give up - to stop doing something you did regularly like a job or sport or even a bad habit like smoking.

Examiner:

What kinds of foods are most popular in your country?

Candidate:

Traditionally people have eaten a lot of cured meats and you still find it on many restaurant menus. I've virtually given up eating them, however, because it's not particularly healthy.

Hang out - to spend time with someone or groups of friends casually.

Examiner:

What do you usually do for leisure or entertainment in your free time?

Candidate:

Sometimes I go to the cinema or a restaurant but most of the time I just hang out with friends at one of our homes. It has the advantage of being both fun and inexpensive.

Keep up with - to make an effort to maintain contact with friends or relatives in circumstances when it might be difficult.

Examiner:

Have you ever thought about moving to a different place?

Candidate:

I've thought about it because job opportunities would be so much better in my capital city. But the big problem for me is that it is so far away, and it would be very difficult to keep up with my family and friends. They are more important to me than a fancy job.

Look after - to take care of a person and make sure they have the things they need, especially a child or sick person. (**Take care of** has a similar meaning)

Examiner:

If you were married, how many children would you choose to have and why?

Candidate:

Well, I grew up in a large family and I would love to have lots of kids of my own. But I think it's more difficult now because for economic reasons both parents have to work. When I was young my mother stayed at home to look after us because in those days one salary was enough to support a large family.

Look back - to review or think about events in the past.

Examiner:

Did you enjoy your time at school when you were very young?

Candidate:

I don't think you necessarily realise when you are a young child how fortunate you are in many ways. If you had asked me at the time, I'm sure I would have complained about lots of things at my school. It's only when you look back that you appreciate what fun it was most of the time. All I remember now was being surrounded by friends in a very caring and joyful environment.

Look forward - to anticipate with pleasure something good that is going to happen.

Examiner:
Do you think it's important to travel during your holidays?

Candidate:

I always look forward to my holidays whether I travel or stay at home. Ideally, I would love to travel abroad and experience new places and cultures during every break from work, but it's not possible for financial reasons. And so I try to use my time productively during my holidays at home and visit local attractions and places of interest.

Look into - to investigate or try to find out the facts about something by getting all the necessary information.

Examiner:
Does your name have any special meaning?

Candidate:
That's an interesting question and to be honest I don't really know. It's quite a common name in my country and I've never given much thought to its origins. Perhaps I should look into it.

Look up - to try to find out information about something from a book, the internet or other records.

Examiner:
What do you do on the internet?

Candidate:
I do a number of things such as stay in contact with my friends and family through social media and read the latest news stories. Primarily, however, it's an invaluable reference tool and I use it to look up the information I need for my studies.

Look up to - to respect or admire somebody because they have more knowledge or experience than you.

Examiner:

When you were in school did any of your teachers have a strong influence on you?

Candidate:

I was lucky in my high school because we had some excellent teachers, but one really stands out. He was my English teacher and was great in motivating us to want to succeed in learning the language. I really looked up to him and he influenced my desire to study the subject at college.

Make sure - to verify or be certain that something is the way you want or expect it to be.

Examiner:

Where do you like to go swimming?

Candidate:

Undoubtedly my favourite place to swim is in the ocean because it's far more invigorating and interesting than swimming in a pool. There is a great beach not too far from my home and I often go at weekends when the conditions are right. You need to make sure that the tides and currents are favourable otherwise swimming can be dangerous.

Make up - to invent a story in order to deceive someone such as lying to the police. Alternatively inventing a story for positive reasons, for example in order to entertain a child.

Examiner:

What do you think are the benefits of reading stories to young children?

Candidate:

I think there are huge benefits. My mother used to read to me every evening before I went to bed and I think it built my language skills and improved my attention. She also made up fairy stories which I loved, and I think they helped to develop my imagination and creative skills at an early age.

Pick out - to choose one particular thing from a group

Examiner:

Do you like shopping for clothes or other goods on the internet?

Candidate:

I wouldn't necessarily say that I enjoy doing it. I shop on the internet primarily because it is usually less expensive. The disadvantage with clothes is that you can't really appreciate what the clothes will really look like. And so I sometimes go to a shop to pick out exactly what I want and then try to find out if it's available cheaper on the internet.

Point out - to tell somebody something he or she needs to know because it is important in a particular situation.

Examiner:

What tourist attractions are there in your hometown?

Candidate:

We do have an attractive park in the centre of the city and the historic cathedral is quite interesting from an architectural point of view. Apart from that, there isn't very much apart from a small art gallery. In fairness, I ought to point out that there are other cities in my country which an average tourist would enjoy far more.

Put away - to save or store something for later use, especially money.

Examiner:

What would be your dream holiday?

Candidate:

It's always been India and I have already started to make plans and put away money for the trip. There are some astonishingly beautiful buildings and landscapes and I adore Indian food. Above all, I'm fascinated by religion and spirituality and in India, both are a major part of everyday life.

Put off - to postpone doing something until later because you are unable or unwilling to do it now.

Examiner:

Do you have a car?

Candidate:

Unfortunately, I don't, and I would love to because it would be so convenient for my work right now. The main reason I don't, well actually it's the only reason, is because I don't have a driver's license. I wish I had learned when I was younger, but I kept putting it off because of the expense of having lessons. I regret that now.

Put up with - to tolerate or accept an unpleasant or inconvenient situation.

Examiner:

Do you like visitors coming to your home?

Candidate:

Most of the time I do, and we have some great friends who come and spend an evening with us. Both of us enjoy socialising and I like having long conversations with groups of people about the latest films and books. Some of our friends have little children now who can be a bit noisy and disruptive, but I put up with it. I can't expect them to leave them at home and get a babysitter.

Run across - to find somebody or something by chance

Examiner:

What do young people in your hometown like to do in their free time?

Candidate:

Well, apart from going to the cinema or walking in the parks, most young people enjoy congregating in the little coffee shops which are on almost every street in the town. They are very informal places and lots of young people do a tour of two or three in the evening. Each tends to specialise in a different snack, so you can eat lots of interesting things and you are bound to run across your friends sooner or later.

Run out - if something runs out, there is no more of it left.

Examiner:

What changes would you like to make to your morning routine?

Candidate:

Well, to be honest, there's only one change I would like to make and that is to get out of bed as soon as the alarm goes off. I have an unfortunate tendency to hit the snooze button a few times. And then inevitably I run out of time to have a proper breakfast before I have to dash out of the house for my train.

Take over - to assume control or take charge of something

Examiner:
Do you enjoy your job?

Candidate:
I enjoy it very much and I also find it quite challenging. I've recently taken over a small team and it's the first time that I've had people directly reporting to me. Initially, it was quite daunting but developing leadership skills is something that I am finding very worthwhile and fulfilling.

Think back - to recall or think about things that happened in the past.

Examiner:
What part of your secondary school education did you enjoy the most?

Candidate:
When I think back on my school days my happiest memories are of my science lessons, particularly chemistry and physics. I just found both subjects totally fascinating and I loved doing experiments. I was lucky that my teachers were so inspirational, and they motivated me to consider becoming a scientist.

Track down - to find something or somebody after making a lot of effort.

Examiner:
Do you spend a lot of money on clothes?

Candidate:
Well, my mother certainly thinks that I do but in reality, I don't think I spend much more than most of my friends. What I will admit to is spending a lot of time clothes shopping. I'm very particular about what I wear, and everything has to be just right. I can easily visit a dozen shops before I track down a pair of jeans or a jumper that I think suits me perfectly.

Try out - to use something for the first time to see whether you like it.

Examiner:
What do you like to cook?

Candidate:
I love cooking all kinds of food, especially Indian cuisine. I'm mainly vegetarian so I like to try out different combinations of spices with lentils and beans. I'm also happy to have a go at traditional Italian dishes because I like using fresh herbs.

Work out - to think carefully about something in order to make a decision.

Examiner:
What are your plans when you leave university?

Candidate:
That's a very good question and I wish I had an easy answer. At the moment I have a number of options and I'm trying to work out what would be best for me in the long term. Certainly, in the short term, it would be best to find a job as quickly as possible, but I'm also tempted to stay on for a master's degree. In the long run that might be better for my career prospects.

APPENDIX TWO - FIFTY USEFUL IDIOMS

The questions in this appendix are all taken from IELTS part three. In addition to looking at how the idiom has been incorporated into the answer please also take note of the use of the more complex grammatical structures and cohesive devices.

An accident waiting to happen

This is a potentially harmful situation that could have been foreseen and thus avoided.

Examiner:
What problems can people have on holiday in a foreign country?

Candidate:
Many big cities that attract lots of tourists also attract the type of people who will take advantage of the fact that these travellers often carry large amounts of money and expensive items like cameras. A friend of mine was recently in Rome on a crowded bus from the airport to the city centre and he had his wallet in his back pocket. It was an accident waiting to happen. It was sadly inevitable that the wallet wasn't there when he got off the bus. There are also potential communication problems if you don't make at least some effort to learn some basic phrases in the local language. You could possibly cause offence by appearing to be impolite or get totally lost if you don't understand directions. Perhaps the most minor problem is that you might order something in a restaurant that you really dislike.

Have an ace up your sleeve

This is to have an effective resource that you keep hidden until you have to use it.

Examiner:
Do you think it's important to have a sense of humour?

Candidate:
Absolutely and perhaps especially so for people in high-powered jobs like business leaders. I worked as an intern in an investment bank when I left university and it was quite a high-pressure environment full of people with big egos. The director of my department was really effective in his job, not just because he had the usual leadership skills but also because he had a great sense of humour. I've seen him in meetings trying to keep control of heated discussions. His best tool was a witty and amusing remark. Getting everybody to laugh is a

great way to calm tensions. Humour was definitely the ace up his sleeve.

An Achilles heel

This is a person's vulnerable, and usually only, weak spot.

Examiner:
Do you think high schools should have more practical classes such as cooking and learning to drive?

Candidate:
I think this is an excellent idea. In addition to the two you mention I would have definitely benefitted from classes in money management. Obviously, we did mathematics, but they didn't teach us enough practical applications of the subject. I recently took out a loan to buy a car and I was baffled by all the options available. Personal finance is something of an Achilles heel for me and a lesson at school on how to compare interest rates would have been really beneficial.

Across the board

Meaning applying to everyone.

Examiner:
Why are elected politicians often so unpopular?

Candidate:
Well certainly in my country politics is quite polarised. The two main political parties each appeal to separate sections of society, one to business and wealthier people and the other primarily to blue-collar workers and organised labour. Inevitably when one of these parties gets into power the policies, they enact favour only one group in society often at the expense of the other. So, for example, tax cuts only for the most wealthy. Personally, I believe that if you are going to either raise or lower taxes it should be across the board. That would be much fairer and wouldn't alienate half the population.

Up in the air

This is a situation that is still to be settled or remains unresolved

Examiner:

What job would you like when you have completed all your studies?

Candidate:

To be honest it's still up in the air. My head tells me that I ought to go into finance and join a bank or an accountancy firm. But my heart tells me to become a teacher. I have had some experience teaching maths and I loved every minute. And I have also been told that I am quite good at it. But it all comes down to money. Teaching, as a profession, is really badly paid in my country. I know they say that money isn't everything but it's really important if you want to raise a family. I think you have to think of your own children just as much as other people's.

In the final analysis

When everything has been considered.

Examiner:

Which method of travel do you consider the safest and why?

Candidate:

Statistically, I have been led to believe that flying is the safest form of transport. All the evidence points in that direction. My problem is that I really don't like flying. It's not that I'm terrified but I'm just uncomfortable when I'm in the air. I think it has to do with a lack of control. Your safety is entirely in the hands of other people. I know that taking a long car journey is far less safe but, for me, it doesn't actually feel like that. And I think it's because I'm largely responsible for my own safety when I'm at the wheel. I know it's illogical, but we don't always act logically.

Up the ante

Increase what is at stake

Examiner:

How has technology changed the way we work?

Candidate:

Once upon a time, it was quite easy just to walk into a job and this was especially true of

blue-collar work. Certainly, in my home city, you didn't need to have passed loads of exams because there was always work in factories. There was a huge car plant that was always hiring people and many of my school friends just walked into jobs there straight out of school. But it's all changed now. The factory is still there but it's largely automated with robots doing all the repetitive tasks. They still need people, but technology has upped the ante. You now need strong IT skills to work there.

Keeping up appearances

To act as though everything is normal or good during times of difficulty.

Examiner:
Do you think that famous people are generally happier than ordinary people?

Candidate:
Well, if you read the glossy magazines you might certainly think so. My grandmother buys one which specialises in photographs of celebrities having a wonderful time in exotic locations. You know the sort of thing, soap stars relaxing on tropical beaches. But I think the reality can sometimes be very different and famous people face all the same sorts of problems that we do, perhaps more so when it comes to personal relationships. Recently my grandmother's magazine had pictures of a celebrity footballer and his wife in their new mansion. But they were just keeping up appearances because shortly after they had a messy and acrimonious divorce.

An article of faith

A firmly held belief

Examiner:
Have attitudes to marriage changed in recent years?

Candidate:
Until comparatively recently in my country, it was an article of faith that marriage was a good thing. All young people were under pressure to get married, settle down and have children. It was quite a conservative culture and any deviations from societal norms were frowned on. But things have changed massively, and I think it's because travel is so much easier now than it used to be. Young people go off to explore other countries and they see other cultures and ways of living. They no longer want their lives to be totally mapped out

when they hit twenty. Marriage is now something that can wait, indefinitely in some cases.

Add insult to injury

To make an unfavourable situation worse

Examiner:
How easy is it to travel around your country?

Candidate:
I think that there are two senses in which travel can be either easy or difficult. In the sense that there are more options then I would say that travel in my country has become increasingly effortless in recent years. The trains are faster and more efficient and there are now more motorways linking the major centres of population. The problem is that transport has become more expensive and in that sense, it is not easy for many people to have the opportunity to travel. Rail journeys used to be heavily subsidised but now, because the operating company has to be profitable, fares have gone up. And to add insult to injury the government has put up the tolls on all the motorways. So using your car instead of the train is not a cheaper alternative.

At the drop of a hat

Instantly or without hesitation

Examiner:
How has the internet changed the way we live?

Candidate:
I think it's a given that the internet has fundamentally changed so many aspects of our lives. For me, it has revolutionised travel. Back in my parent's day, it was actually quite a tedious task to organise a holiday and it was also very time-consuming. I remember that they used to spend hours on the phone organising flight tickets and then even more time booking hotels. Admittedly they could have gone to a travel agent and got them to organise a package deal but even that meant a trip into town. Now you barely have to plan ahead. If you unexpectedly have a few days free you can book everything online and you can be on a weekend break in a foreign city at the drop of a hat.

Go back to the drawing board

When something fails, and you have to start from the beginning

Examiner:

Do you agree that we learn best from our mistakes?

Candidate:

I definitely do agree with that and believe that we shouldn't always think in terms of mistakes as failures because they don't have to be. It's inevitable that all of us will make mistakes from time to time but as long as you learn from those mistakes and don't repeat them then they become valuable life experiences. They definitely are not failures. Life, to a certain extent, is a series of experiments and inevitably some of those experiments won't go according to plan. You just need to go back to the drawing board and, using what you have learned, try again until you get it right.

The ball is in your court

When it is up to you to make the next step or decision
(Note that it may also be his/her/their court etc.)

Examiner:

What life experience do you wish you had gained?

Candidate:

Well, something that I regret that I didn't do when I left school was to spend a year abroad. Some of my university friends travelled around either Africa or Asia and a couple went as far as Australia. They all have amazing stories of the people that they met and the adventures they had. I know that some people, my parents in particular, just think that these gap years are just an excuse for a year-long holiday, but I think that it can bring important benefits. It can make you more resilient and self-reliant and being exposed to other cultures is beneficial for your personal growth. To be honest, I'm considering doing it when I leave university instead of going straight into a job. The ball's in my court I suppose.

Barking up the wrong tree

Looking in the wrong place or pursuing the wrong thing or path

Examiner:

Do you believe everything you read in the newspapers?

Candidate:

Okay, I think I can give a very definite 'no' in response to this question. We are lucky in my country that we have, supposedly, a totally free press but virtually all of our newspapers are owned by very wealthy individuals. And they use those newspapers to further their own interests, particularly their business interests. The editorial techniques they use are quite subtle and it very often amounts to no more than choosing to ignore some stories or giving prominence to others. But often the editors distort the truth to suit a particular agenda. I think that if you really want to know what is going on in your country then you have to read widely and from a number of sources. If you think that you can get all the news you need from one newspaper, then you're barking up the wrong tree.

Be glad to see the back of something or someone

Be happy when a situation is at an end or a person leaves.

Examiner:

At what age should people retire from work?

Candidate:

Well in my country the official retirement age is 67, that's the age at which you can collect your state pension if you are entitled to one. And most people do seem to finish work at that age. But I think it should really depend upon your state of health and whether you find your work fulfilling. One of my grandfathers was employed in a factory and he was glad to see the back of it at the age of 67 because he found it quite boring and physically tough. On the other hand, my other grandfather is still working, and I think he's now nearly 70. He loves his work and he's not the sort of person who would adjust well to having lots of time on his hands and without a structured day. And so I think that people should be allowed to retire when they feel ready for it.

Best of both worlds

A situation in which a person can get the advantages of two different or contrasting things at the same time

Examiner:

Do you prefer advice from your family or from your friends?

Candidate:

To be honest I think that both sources of advice can be valuable, but you need to bear in

mind that although your parents and your friends think that they have your best interests at heart they sometimes have a hidden agenda. My father, for example, really wanted me to study law at university and he gave me lots of advice which highlighted all the positives. But having a son as a lawyer was something felt he could be very proud of and I'm sure that influenced his advice. My girlfriend at the time, on the other hand, didn't want me to go to university at all because she didn't want me to move away. She kept emphasising how expensive a degree would be. And so I think that if you listen to advice from both your family and your friends, bearing in mind that they might not be totally objective, then you can have the best of both worlds.

A big fish in a small pond

Somebody who is important but only in a small organisation or company

Examiner:
Would you like to have your own business?

Candidate:
I am aware of the risks and pitfalls of running your own enterprise. Your working hours are potentially very long and the rewards are not necessarily any better than if you were employed by somebody else. If anything, they could be considerably lower. However, what really appeals to me about being my own boss is the independence and not having to answer to anybody. I like the idea of being a big fish in my own small pond.

Bite off more than you can chew

Take on a project that is bigger than you are able to deal with.

Examiner:
How should students spend their summer vacations?

Candidate:
In an ideal world, I think that they should probably go travelling and seek out new experiences. Perhaps they should also spend time revising and consolidating what they have learned during the previous year. But in reality, most have to get a job. We have to take out loans to pay for our university education in my country and most of us are desperately trying to avoid ending up with huge debts at the end of three years. And so we invariably spend the summer working long hours. Last summer I worked in a restaurant almost every night of the week and I spent the days trying to study. To be honest, I think I bit off more than I could chew, and I just ended up being really tired all the time. I certainly

didn't revise very effectively. That's not how a student should spend his or her vacation but sadly it's the reality for most of us.

Blessing in disguise

Something good which is not instantly recognised or a misfortune which turns out to have advantages.

Examiner:
Do you think it is important for a child to have a lot of toys in order to be happy?

Candidate:
I think that I can unreservedly say that it is absolutely not important for a child to have a lot of toys. My parents weren't particularly wealthy when I was growing up and I have four siblings, so it simply wasn't possible for me to have all the latest toys and gadgets. I used to have to make do with battered old things handed down from my brothers. At the time I resented this because some of my friends used to get the most amazing toys at Christmas and birthdays. Now I realise that it was a blessing in disguise. I had to learn to be more creative and resourceful with what I did have. I also learned to value things more because if I broke something, I knew that there wouldn't be a replacement. But above all, I developed a love for reading. Books were always available, and I think it is far better for a child to be reading than playing with the latest fashionable toy.

Can't judge a book by its cover

You are not able to appreciate something just based on appearance

Examiner:
Can clothing tell you much about a person?

Candidate:
Well, they do say that you can't judge a book by its cover and I think that this is true with regards to clothing. In the fairly recent past, you could safely make a number of assumptions about a person's wealth or social status from what they wore. To a certain extent that is still true with regards to somebody's job or profession. In my country, white-collar workers still wear traditional business attire such as suits and manual labourers wear overalls or some sort of boiler suit. But when it comes to clothes for leisure it's unwise to presume anything about a person. People these days, particularly the young, all seem to

wear jeans, trainers and a hoodie irrespective of how much money they have.

Caught between two stools

Fail to achieve either of two contrasting aims or find difficulty in choosing between two alternatives.

Examiner:
How well do you think schools prepare young people for working life?

Candidate:
I don't think they do it particularly well, to be honest, but I also don't think they have much choice in the matter. The problem is that the government imposes a national curriculum and it's biased heavily in favour of quite academic subjects. There's also a system of testing in place which is supposed to ensure that every student is achieving particular intellectual standards every year. At the same time, schools are also supposed to be teaching the practical skills that young people will need in later life, but they simply don't have the resources to do it adequately. Our teachers are caught between two stools trying to do two things and not having sufficient time for either.

Cross that bridge when you come to it

Deal with a problem if and when it arises and not make preparations in advance.

Examiner:
What problems can people face after retirement?

Candidate:
One surprisingly common problem is that some people don't cope very well with having lots of free time. If you have spent years devoted to your work or professional life, then suddenly not having your day mapped out can be quite daunting. Some old people end up sitting in front of the television all the time which is certainly not good for your physical health and possibly your mental health as well. Also, a major problem is that many people don't prepare financially for the day when they no longer have an income from their work. Ideally, you should start putting money by in a personal pension plan when you are in your twenties but at that age, retirement seems a long way off and it's easy to think that you will cross that bridge when you get to it.

Cry over spilt milk

Complain about a misfortune when there is nothing you are able to do about it

Examiner:
Do you agree that we learn best from our mistakes?

Candidate:
There's a saying in my country which translates roughly as, 'The person who never makes a mistake never makes anything.' Essentially it means that it is impossible to be inventive or creative without making errors along the way. The important thing, I suppose, is not to give up and be upset when you fail. There's no point crying over spilt milk. Try to understand exactly why something went wrong, put procedures in place to ensure the mistakes don't happen again and start once more.

Cut corners

Do something inadequately in order to save time or money

Examiner:
What are the pros and cons of low-cost air travel?

Candidate:
Undoubtedly for me, the biggest advantage has been the opportunity to travel to lots of foreign countries and experience different cultures. My parents never had that chance when they were my age because air travel was prohibitively expensive. The low-cost airlines also fly to some less well-known cities and places off the beaten track which gives you the opportunity to explore regions you might not otherwise visit. The main disadvantage I suppose is the lack of personal service and attention to detail. For the tickets to be cheap the low-cost carriers have to cut corners and that can sometimes mean that travelling with them is not always a comfortable or pleasant experience.

Play devil's advocate

To take a side in an argument which is the opposite of what you really believe

Examiner:
Do you think there are any subjects which currently aren't being taught in your schools which should be?

Candidate:

There are a number of practical skills that I would have liked to have learned at school. It's difficult to find good reliable people to fix things around the home like the electrics and plumbing. I wish I could do this myself. Something that is even more important however is critical thinking skills. These are not taught as a specialised subject and we need them more than ever before. So many people read things on the internet and accept them at face value and they don't question the facts or the motives of the people posting these stories. Students should be given the skills to enable them to analyse facts objectively before forming a judgement. They should also know how to play devil's advocate so that they can test their own ideas and establish whether they stand up to scrutiny.

Better the devil you know

It's better to deal with an undesirable situation or person than choose an alternative which might be worse

Examiner:

Do you think it's good to change jobs occasionally?

Candidate:

I think that if you are in a reasonably good well-paid job and are happy with your work then you will be disinclined to change. I believe this is only natural. Many people are risk-averse and have a better the devil you know attitude. Personally, I believe that it's good to try new things and embrace challenging situations like a different workplace. It's important for your personal growth to be able to adapt to new situations, new environments and new people.

Every cloud has a silver lining

All bad situations and negative occurrences will have some positive aspects.

Examiner:

How important is it for school students to do well in all of their exams?

Candidate:

I'm sure that the overwhelming majority of school students want to at least pass and preferably excel in every exam they are obliged to take. Something that my father told me, however, which I found quite reassuring when I was younger and getting stressed at exam time, was that the results of exams become less important the further away in age you are from them. He also said that failing exams isn't necessarily the calamity it might seem at the time. Every cloud has a silver lining and it's entirely possible that failing an exam in one subject will incline you to focus your attention on subjects you really love.

Get cold feet

To lose your nerve or confidence

Examiner:
What do you think of extreme sports such as skydiving or rock climbing?

Candidate:
Extreme sports aren't for me personally and I'm quite risk-averse when it comes to physical activities. I was once supposed to go abseiling with some friends but got cold feet at the last minute. However, I have absolutely no problems with others taking part in exhilarating and possibly dangerous adventure sports. People should be free to make up their own minds about whether the thrills are worth the risks. Having said that I do feel that it is unreasonable when extreme sports fans get into difficulties and expect others to risk their lives to rescue them. Often first responders have to expose themselves to danger and that, I believe, is unnecessary and unreasonable.

Jump on the bandwagon

Join or support, often in an opportunistic way, a growing movement or a currently fashionable activity

Examiner:
What influence can celebrities have on society?

Candidate:
I'm sure that it depends very much on the character and reputation of the celebrity. If, for example, a famous footballer is known for always playing fairly, speaking well of opposing teams and having a respectable private life then people might be inclined to listen to him if he speaks about something unconnected with his sport. So often though celebrities attach themselves to popular causes, like supporting green issues, but you know they are just jumping on the bandwagon. I've heard of rock stars flying on private jets to play at charity concerts which raise money for environmental causes. In those types of instances, I'm sure most people are able to see through the hypocrisy and the celebrity's influence is minimal.

Kill two birds with one stone

To accomplish two different things at the same time.

Examiner:

What should schools do to educate young people about a healthy diet?

Candidate:

In my opinion, I think that there are often two aspects of education for school students. One is the old-fashioned lecture type of lesson. In the context of a healthy diet, you just sit them down, perhaps in a biology lesson, and inform them what proportions of your daily food intake should be made up of protein, fat, and carbohydrate etc. This type of academic approach is okay, but it probably wouldn't stop some students from going off to buy a burger and chips for lunch. The other aspect of education is more functional. Instead of telling students how to do something, you show them. When it comes to nutrition the schools could kill two birds with one stone and provide a healthy meal for lunch and provide a handout detailing what ingredients it contains and why these are good for health.

The last straw

(also *the final straw*)

The last in a series of unpleasant events that finally makes you feel that you cannot continue to accept a disagreeable situation.

Examiner:

Do you think it's good to move to a different employer occasionally?

Candidate:

I certainly believe that it is good to change your employment if there are aspects of your job which are unsatisfactory. There are potentially many of these. For me personally, a few years ago, I became quite unhappy at work for a number of reasons. The people I had to work with weren't team players, nor were they particularly friendly. I also had targets to meet which I felt were unrealistic. But the final straw for me was being passed over for promotion. I felt in those circumstances that I had very little to lose by changing jobs. On the other hand, if you are reasonably happy and your pay and conditions are good, it's probably always best to stay where you are.

Cut a long story short

To get to the point leaving out some of the details.

Examiner:
Do you believe that it is important to be on time?

Candidate:
As far as I'm concerned, I think that it's essential and there are a couple of reasons for this. The first is simply a matter of good manners. I think that it's exceedingly impolite to keep people waiting. Obviously, it's a good plan to be punctual for things like job interviews but that's as much for your benefit as it is for the people waiting to interview you. But even when you are meeting friends on an informal basis, I believe that it's extremely discourteous not to be on time. As far as I'm concerned, it's no excuse to say that you can use your mobile to explain why you are running late. The second reason is purely practical. There can potentially be adverse consequences for being late. On one occasion a few years ago I was careless and didn't leave enough time to get to the airport to catch a flight and, to cut a long story short, I missed it. As a result, I wasn't in time for a friend's wedding.

Miss the boat

To be too slow to take advantage of an opportunity.

Examiner:
If a school student has a talent for sport or the arts, do you think it is better for them to focus on this or academic studies?

Candidate:
I believe that what tends to happen in schools is that parents and teachers invariably emphasise or, even overstate, the importance of academic success. When they think about the future, they consider that good academic results will inevitably lead to a solid, secure and lucrative career. Achieving success in the arts or sports is considerably more difficult and a career in either can be precarious. What often happens is that those students who are truly talented in the arts or sport are not encouraged. Instead, they are told to focus on scholarly pursuits and good exam results. If you are good at a sport or artistic endeavour, and you want to be successful at it in later life, then you need to have a single-minded devotion to it from a young age. If you don't then you will miss the boat and possibly always regret it.

On the ball

When a person is quick-witted and able to respond to new situations and ideas.

Examiner:
What qualities do you think a good teacher should have?

Candidate:
I would say that great teachers need two key attributes. The first is a thorough knowledge of the subject matter they are teaching and ideally, they should also have a passion for it. This is absolutely necessary but not sufficient. I've come across teachers who are experts in their fields but don't have the skills to impart this knowledge to their students. This brings me to the second key attribute which is excellent classroom skills. Teachers need to build a rapport with their students which means they need to be superb communicators. I believe they also need to be flexible and adaptable. Students are unpredictable and if a lesson isn't working, they might need to change direction quickly. They, therefore, need to be on the ball and ready to change what they might have planned.

Once in a blue moon

Very infrequently

Examiner:
Can you suggest how the study of history in school could be made more interesting for students who think it's boring?

Candidate:
I remember very clearly being bored during history lessons at school. I'm convinced that this was because of the method my teacher used. Basically, each lesson was a lecture. He delivered information and we had to make notes. It's probably not surprising that many of us didn't find it interesting. It would have been much better at my school had the teachers made use of resources in our city and the surrounding area. It was only once in a blue moon that we were ever taken outside the classroom but there were numerous museums and historical sites nearby. There were even a couple of locations where important battles had taken place. Looking back it seems to have been a huge missed opportunity that we didn't have some of our history lessons in these places. I think this would really have brought the past to life and history would not have seemed so dull.

Over the top

To an excessive degree

Examiner:

Do you think it's a good idea for parents to start teaching academic skills to their pre-school children?

Candidate:

I do believe that it is useful for parents to teach some basic skills to their children before they go to their first school. My mother, for example, taught me to read when I was very young, and it undoubtedly gave me a head start at junior school. I can't remember if I had any numerical skills at that age but I'm sure that an ability to count would also give you an advantage. I don't believe however that parents should subject their kids to some sort of rigorous academic pre-school programme. You do hear about some competitive parents doing this, but I'm convinced it's totally over the top and might have the opposite effect from what is intended. It's possible that these children might take the opportunity to rebel at the earliest opportunity.

Out of the blue

Totally unexpectedly

Examiner:

In the past 40 years or so, have there been any changes to how often people visit others?

Candidate:

In my experience, there has been a major change in the frequency of visits to and from friends and family. When I was younger and living at home with my parents it was extremely common for people to drop in on people they knew. This was a regular occurrence and such visits were not planned in advance. This, I think, was a throwback to a time when people didn't have telephones. Everybody lived close to his or her friends and relatives, there wasn't much to do in the evenings so wandering a few doors up the road to call on somebody was common. Nowadays, on the other hand, people have much busier lives and tend to live further away from people they know. It's just not practical to turn up at somebody's house out of the blue. They might not be at home for one thing and it's even seen as being impolite not to phone to make arrangements in advance. As a result, people don't visit friends so often.

Pass the buck

To shift the responsibility for something to someone else

Examiner:
What qualities does a successful self-employed businessperson need to have?

Candidate:
My father ran a small business and I saw at first-hand what traits you need to make a success of it. Primarily, I think you need to be totally flexible. You don't have just one clearly defined job, instead, you have lots of duties and responsibilities. Also, there's nowhere to pass the buck. As a self-employed business owner, you're the one who will have to deal with whatever problems arise and find solutions. In addition, you have to be prepared to put in a constant and consistent effort. You can't phone in sick and, in the case of my father, you can only rarely take holidays. If you don't go to work, you don't get paid. Finally, I think you have to be able to deal with uncertainty. Your income can fluctuate from month to month, so you have to keep a clear head and not panic when things aren't going so well.

See eye to eye

When two people agree totally on something
(can also be in the negative - *we don't see eye to eye*)

Examiner:
What are some reasons why friends sometimes lose contact with each other?

Candidate:
I think that one of the main reasons these days why friends might find it difficult to keep in touch is simply because people are far more mobile than they used to be. When I think back to my friends in high school, very few still live in the town where we all grew up. We all went to different universities and then to different cities and even countries to find work. Keeping in touch in those circumstances is problematic. Another explanation is that people change. Different life experiences are likely to result in us having a different worldview. I've found that I simply don't see eye to eye with some former friends about such things as politics or religion. We no longer have the same things in common and being with them simply isn't as enjoyable as it used to be.

Set in your ways

Not wanting to change a fixed habit or routine.

Examiner:
Do you think elderly people can easily adapt to a new environment?

Candidate:
My grandparents recently downsized. They had been living in a large house with a garden and the upkeep was becoming too much for them. It was time-consuming and expensive. It was also a long way from a supermarket. And so they bought a small apartment in the centre of their nearby town close to shops and local amenities. The family thought they would find it difficult to adapt but, in fact, they have never been happier. They love being able to walk everywhere and they have a lot more time. They might not be typical, of course, but I believe that the usual image of old people being set in their ways and not willing to embrace change is not always accurate. They can just as easily adapt to a new environment as younger people.

Sit on the fence

To avoid making a decision or avoid taking sides in an argument.

Examiner:
Do you think schools should include the teaching of decision-making skills in the curriculum?

Candidate:
It sounds like an excellent idea. Schools should definitely help students develop their confidence and independence and an important part of that is teaching them how to make sensible and independent choices. When you are young you don't have to make many important decisions, most are made for you, but as soon as you hit eighteen you are bombarded with choices you have to make. You can get expert help to decide such things as what university course to take but there are many others, like choosing who to date, which are intensely personal and only you can decide. Making the wrong decision or just sitting on the fence can have negative long-term consequences so having the skills to weigh up the pros and cons can be hugely beneficial.

Taken aback

This idiom is invariably used in the passive as in, *I was taken aback*. It means that you were shocked or surprised by something.

Examiner:
Why are some sports fans so passionate?

Candidate:
Well, I must admit that I was taken aback when I last went to a football match and witnessed just how emotional the fans were getting. I think it's because some sports, and football, in particular, have very deep roots in local communities. And over the years very deep-seated rivalries can develop. It's almost a tribal thing. It's not just one team playing against another team but one city battling with an ancient rival. And these passions can be even stronger when one country is playing another at football. I think it is appalling when these emotions turn into violence but, to a certain extent, it is understandable, particularly if the two countries have had a tempestuous history.

Take it with a grain of salt
(alternatively, *a pinch of salt*)

To not believe something you are told because you think it is unlikely to be true.

Examiner:
Some people say that technology will replace humans in the workplace. Do you agree?

Candidate:
Claims about robots and computers replacing humans in factories in offices and workplaces have been made for a long time now and I tend to take these with a pinch of salt. It's certainly true that a lot of repetitive manual tasks of the type you typically see on production lines can be done by robots. It's also the case that computers have reduced the need for people to perform many routine clerical tasks in offices. But in reality, automation results in the creation of new categories of work such as customer service or software design. Robots will take away our boring jobs but there will always be a need for highly skilled humans in the workplace.

Rule of thumb

A principle with a broad application not meant to be totally accurate.

Examiner:
Do you think it would be a good investment for a local person living in a tourist area to open a shop to sell souvenirs?

Candidate:
As a general rule of thumb, if you are living in an area with lots of tourists, it is usually considered a good idea to start a business that targets them. In this city, lots of people have, for example, started doing Airbnb. The assumption is that tourists have lots of money and are happy to spend it. What people don't necessarily consider however is that tourists are quite discriminating. They won't automatically eat in a restaurant just because it claims to serve traditional local cuisine. They will read the TripAdvisor reviews and consider a number of places to eat. I believe it is the same with souvenir shops. Tourists won't just come flocking to your shop and spend money. Your mementos will have to be authentic and good value and browsing in your shop will have to be a more pleasant experience than in any rival establishments. I suspect that making money from tourists is not as easy as people tend to imagine.

Better late than never

It's better to do something late than not to do it at all

Examiner:
In your country, besides universities, are there any other places or institutions where adults can study?

Candidate:
I'm really delighted that adult education is considered to be important in my country and we do have colleges which specialise in courses for adults who have other demands on their time such as a career or childcare. The classes are therefore usually in the evening or at weekends. Many libraries also offer guided study facilities for adults. Adult education used to be considered a 'better late than never' option. In other words, you would study something in later life which you might not have had the opportunity to study when you were young. Nowadays the emphasis is more on lifelong learning and it's great that there are places where you can continue your education after you have left school or university.

Call it a day

To stop doing something, especially work or other regular activity.

> Examiner:
> *Can you suggest why some people prefer to work from home?*

> Candidate:
> *I have a friend who works from home and she is very enthusiastic about it. Some of the reasons are quite trivial, for example, she likes the fact that she can wear comfortable informal clothes and have her cat sitting on her knee. And nobody knows if she eats pastries in the middle of the morning. On a more serious note, she has saved a fortune in travel costs. But what really appreciates is the fact that she can organise her working schedule around her other commitments. When she worked in an office, she couldn't really leave in the middle of the afternoon without there being raised eyebrows. Now she can get up very early to do her work and then, assuming she has finished it, call it a day at three in the afternoon. This leaves her time to pursue other interests.*

To make it up as you go along

To improvise continuously rather than planning in advance.

> Examiner:
> *To what extent do you think people should plan their foreign holiday before they go?*

> Candidate:
> *I'm sure that it's a good idea to plan the basics. At the very least I like to book my accommodation in advance. I have some friends who just buy a plane ticket to somewhere and then make it up as they go along. They make enquiries about hotels when they land at their destination which means that they sometimes end up staying at some very interesting places. I don't like this degree of uncertainty but at the same time, I don't want every moment of my holiday to be arranged before I leave. Some people like to know exactly what they will be doing each day, but I enjoy a degree of spontaneity when I am on holiday.*

It's not rocket science

It's not difficult to do or understand.

Examiner:
Do you think it's a good idea for people to grow some of their own food at home, if possible?

Candidate:
I'm convinced that it's a wonderful idea. Nothing quite tastes the same as home-grown produce and most fruit and vegetables are much sweeter and more succulent when they are freshly picked. You know that your produce has not been pumped full of pesticides and it can also save you a lot of money. Supermarket fruit can be quite expensive. I also know from experience that it's easy to do and very satisfying. Growing your own isn't rocket science and you don't need a big garden. I grow herbs in pots in my kitchen and tomatoes in a window box. I can thoroughly recommend it.

So far so good

An expression of satisfaction with progress made.

Examiner:
Do you think that if you want to play a musical instrument well you need to start learning when you are young?

Candidate:
I'm sure it's probably true that if you want to be a professional musician you need to start when you are a child. You hear about child prodigies who start playing the violin or piano when they are four or five and then go on to have careers with the great orchestras of the world. But to be honest, very few of us will ever be able to do that no matter how early we start. I'm sure you have to have an innate talent for it. Most of us want to learn an instrument just for fun and for the satisfaction of being able to do it. It doesn't necessarily matter if nobody ever listens to us. I started to play the guitar a couple of years ago and, so far so good. I play it well enough to amuse myself even if I don't amuse anybody else.

Roll up your sleeves

Be prepared to work hard at something.

Examiner:

Many small businesses fail after just a year or two. Can you suggest why that is?

Candidate:

I have a feeling that a lack of proper preparation might be the main reason for small business failure. If you are going to be successful you need to know your market inside out. Not only do you need to research who your likely customers are, what they want and what they are prepared to pay but you must also know the strengths and weaknesses of your competitors. I'm also sure that it's more expensive than people imagine starting a business. In the first few months, your outgoings are likely to exceed your income and you need sufficient funds to keep yourself afloat before you start making a profit. And last, but not least, you need to be ready for some seriously hard work. You need to roll up your sleeves and be ready for long hours. Running your own business is not a nine-to-five job.

AND FINALLY

One of the great things about my job is that I get to speak to students of all ages from around the world -albeit mostly by Skype. They come from a huge variety of backgrounds and cultures and all have some amazing personal stories to tell.

However, what they share in common is a dream. For some, it is to study abroad and for others, it is to work in a professional field such as engineering, medicine or accounting. And then there are those who are seeking a better life in another country.

For these dreams to come true they require a high band score in IELTS and nothing gives me greater pleasure than helping them to achieve that goal.

Whatever your dreams are, I very much hope this book helps you accomplish them, and I wish you the very best of luck.

I would love to hear your stories so please do contact me.

Charles

charles.hooton@oxfordalumni.org

charleshooton.com

Printed in Great Britain
by Amazon

40674528R00137